SHÍYÒNG HÀNYǓ XIĚZUÒ JÌNJIĒ
实用汉语写作进阶

Practical Chinese Writing

(中级)
(Secondary)

华文盛世 编著

First Edition 2011

ISBN 978-7-119-06860-2
© Foreign Languages Press Co. Ltd, Beijing, China, 2011
Published by Foreign Languages Press Co. Ltd
24 Baiwanzhuang Road, Beijing 100037, China
http://www.flp.com.cn   E-mail: flp@cipg.org.cn
Distributed by China International Book Trading Corporation
35 Chegongzhuang Xilu, Beijing 100044, China
P.O. Box 399, Beijing, China
Printed in the People's Republic of China

编写说明

　　为适应对外汉语写作教学的新特点,本册教材在编写过程中,突出了对外汉语写作教材的趣味性、可读性、简明性、可操作性等特点,旨在切实提升学生的汉语写作能力。本教材每篇课文分为"要点提示""例文指路""结构模板""练习"几个部分,全书体例统一,结构简明、易教、易学。

　　"要点提示"部分明确该课学习的目的和重点,做到目标明确、重点突出、难易适中。

　　"例文指路"部分所选例文涵盖了现代汉语的常用体裁,学生在日常生活、学习、工作中会经常用到,因此学生在学习这些篇章时会感到具有现实针对性和可操作性。所选篇章篇幅适中,语言较规范,浅显易读。在例文的注释中,编者对每种现代汉语写作体裁的用途,以及结构中每部分的具体写法、写作内容、语言特点、惯用语等方面,都作了详细说明,通过学习学生能轻松地把握日常生活中各种文体的写法。

　　"结构模板"部分,对所选例文的结构、格式作了"模式化"总结,使学生对每篇文章的结构、格式一目了然。同时在注释中还有较为详细的"模板结构说明",对每篇文章写作格式中的每项要素的安排都分别作出了说明。这部分也是本教材的一大特点,可帮助学生克服在汉语写作中普遍面临的可操作性差的难题。

　　"练习"部分设计了"照猫画虎""顺藤摘瓜""病例诊断""例文评析"等题目。练习的题目在名称设计上突出趣味性,练习内容上突出循序渐进原则,每课课后的练习先易后难,又与"例文指路""结构模板"紧密联系,学生能够边学边用、学以致用,在短时间内掌握各种体裁的结构、格式、内容、语言等特点,大大提升了学生汉语写作的水平。

Of Compilation

　　In order to adapt to the new characteristics of teaching writing in Chinese as a foreign language, this textbook focuses on the palatability, readability, simplicity, adaptability and other characteristics of teaching to achieve its aim of improving the Chinese writing ability of all students.

　　Every text in this book has been divided into four sections: Basic principles and aims, Example guide, Structure templates and Exercises. The whole book has a clear and unified structure, that is simple to teach, and easy to learn.

The "Basic principles and aims" clarifies the aims and the areas of emphasis of the text, setting out achievable goals of the lesson.

The "Example guide" provides practical examples of common modern Chinese phrases that can be used by students in their daily activities, studies and work. The lengths of the chosen examples are short, and the language they contain is easy to understand and read. The supplementary notes included in this section detail the purpose and style of modern Chinese writing, as well as its composition, language characteristics, idioms and other structural parts, making it easy for students to understand the style of Chinese writing.

The "Structure templates" creates a structure and format for the chosen examples, and gives students the ability to identify the structural format of passages at a glance. There are also more detailed structural template descriptions in the supplementary notes, that directly illuminate the structural arrangement of each separate article. This is a feature of this textbook which helps students overcome the commonly faced difficulties attached to learning to write Chinese.

The "Exercises" section contains many different types of exercises for students, such as Follow the model, Follow the templates, Case of illness diagnosis, Diagnostic conclusion etc. The exercises progress from easy to difficult and are related to the Example guide and Structure templates. Through the exercises students can study the practical applications of the language they have learned, as well as mastering the characteristics of the various structures, formats and contents of the paragraphs they encounter, which will enable them to master Chinese writing quickly and easily.

目 录
Contents

第 一 课　便　　条 ··· 1
　　　　　　Note

第 二 课　请　　柬 ··· 8
　　　　　　Invitation

第 三 课　日　　记 ··· 17
　　　　　　Diary

第 四 课　启　　事 ··· 23
　　　　　　Notice

第 五 课　介 绍 信 ··· 31
　　　　　　Letter of Introduction

第 六 课　求 职 信 ··· 35
　　　　　　Letter of Application

第 七 课　申 请 书 ··· 41
　　　　　　Application

第 八 课　贺　　信 ··· 48
　　　　　　Letter of Congratulation

第 九 课　履　　历 ··· 54
　　　　　　Resume

第 十 课　海　　报 ··· 59
　　　　　　Poster

第十一课　欢 迎 词 ··· 65
　　　　　　Welcome Speech

第十二课　一般书信 ··· 70
　　　　　　Ordinary Letter

第十三课　倡 议 书 ··· 76
　　　　　　Proposal

第十四课 演讲稿 ··· 84
　　　　　Speech Manuscript

第十五课 邀请函 ··· 94
　　　　　Invitation Letter

第十六课 感谢信 ··· 104
　　　　　Thank-you Letter

第一课　便条
Note

Basic principles and aims
要点提示

1. 了解便条的基本用途、写作格式。
   Understand the basic purpose and writing format of notes.
2. 掌握便条写作中语言、措词的基本特点。
   Master the basic knowledge of language and wording in note writing.
3. 基本掌握便条的写法。
   Master the basics of note writing.

例文一

Example I

请假条①

王老师：②

　　我昨晚着凉发烧了，身体不适，今天不能到校学习，请准假一天。③

　　此致

敬礼④

　　　　　　　　　　　学生　李明

写法注释
Writing notes

① 用途：如果发生了突然的意外事情，不能去上学、上班或参加某项活动，向有关负责人请假时要使用请假条。

② 称谓：写明收条人的称呼，要用敬语，一般不能直呼其名。

③ 正文：正文内容要简明扼要，写明请假的理由，请假的天数等。理由要充分，用词注意多使用一

1

二〇一〇年三月十日 ⑤

Application for Leave

Mr. Wang:

  I caught a cold, had a fever, and felt uncomfortable last night, so I am unable to attend school today. Please grant me an extension of leave for a day.

  Best Wishes!

Student Li Ming
March 10th, 2010

些敬语,如请、希望、企请、恳请等。

④ **文末敬语**：一般使用"此致、敬礼"等固定用语。

⑤ **署名**：本部分有两项内容,要写明请假人的姓名和请假的时间。在姓名前要写上与收条人的关系,如学生×××、职员×××等。

① Purpose: If an unexpected event or accident occurs, and you cannot attend school, work or another activity and need to apply for leave, you should use the "Application for Leave".

② Appellation: Write the recipient's name clearly, usually using an honorific title, as you generally do not refer to the recipient by their first name.

③ Text: The text should be written concisely and briefly, containing the reason, and the number of days of leave being applied for, all written in a polite form using terms like "please, wish, look forward to, expect" etc.

④ Honorific at the end of the note: Usually such phrases as 此致,敬礼 are used to end this type of note.

⑤ Signature: This part has two components, the author's name and the date the note was written, both of which should be written clearly. The name should always come after the appellation, such as student ××× or employee ×××.

例文二
Example II

留言条①

李主任：②

今天上午九点，我来办事处找您办理出国留学有关事宜，不巧您正好外出开会不在。下午三点我再来，请您在办公室等我。③

此致
敬礼④

黄浩

二○一○年四月五日⑤

Message

Director Li,

I came to your office this morning at nine o'clock to ask you to handle the matters related to studying abroad, but you were unfortunately out at a meeting. I will return at three o'clock this afternoon, please wait for me in your office.

Best Wishes!

Huang Hao

April 5th, 2010

写法注释
Writing notes

① **用途**：如果有事找人办理或交谈，对方不在，又不能久等，使用留言条。有时替代别人接了电话，或代别人商洽了某事，怕事后忘记，也可以使用留言条，转告对方。

② **称呼**：写明收条人的称呼，要用敬语或称其职务，一般不能直呼其名。

③ **正文**：正文内容写作时要简明扼要，写明来访的目的、事由、时间。如果必须当面办理，还要把约定面谈的时间、地点写明，便于对方有所准备。

④ **文末敬语**：一般使用"此致、敬礼"等固定用语。

⑤ **署名**：本部分有两项内容，要写明来访者的姓名和来访的时间。

① Purpose: If you have something you want to ask someone to do or to talk to them about, but cannot wait for a long time for them to return, you can leave them a message. Sometimes, when answering calls for someone or discussing matters for other people you can take down messages for them, so as not to forget what has been discussed.

② Appellation: Write the recipient's name clearly, usually using an honorific title, as you generally do not refer to the recipient by their first name.

③ Text: The text should be written

concisely and briefly, containing the reason and time of visiting. If it is a matter that must be handled face to face, you should clearly suggest a future time and place to meet so that the recipient may prepare for the meeting.

④ Honorific at the end of the note: Usually such phrases as 此致, 敬礼 are used to end this type of message.

⑤ Signature: This part has two components, the author's name and the time and date the message was written, both of which should be written clearly.

生 词
New words

着凉	zháoliáng	catch a cold
敬礼	jìnglǐ	best wishes
办事处	bànshìchù	office
留学	liúxué	study abroad
事宜	shìyí	matter
办公室	bàngōngshì	office

结构模板
The template of structure

　　　　　　　　　　□□□①

□□□:②

　　□□。③

　　此致

敬　礼④

第一课 便条

□□：□□□
□□□□年□□月□□日 ⑤

模板格式说明

The template format explanation

① 标题：要写明"请假条"或"留言条"等字样，位置居中。

Caption: Write 请假条 or 留言条 at the top centre.

② 称谓：要顶格写上收条人的称谓，后面要加上冒号。

Appellation: Write the recipient's name without indenting, follow it with a colon.

③ 正文：在称谓之下，首行要空两格，正文内容要注意正确使用标点符号。

Text: There should be two spaces between the left margin and the first line of the text. Make sure that you are using the correct punctuation.

④ 文末敬语："此致"前空两格，"敬礼"在"此致"下行，要顶格。

Honorific at the end: 此致 should be written with two spaces before it, and 敬礼 should be written on the line below, with no spaces preceding it.

⑤ 署名：在"敬礼"的下一行写明留条人姓名，位置在便条的右下方，姓名之下写明时间，一般要使用汉字形式。

Signature: The author's name should be written on the right hand side of the page, on the line below 敬礼. The date of the message should be written under the name, and is usually written in the Chinese format.

 练习
Exercises

1 照猫画虎
Follow the model

按照上面提示的例文结构模板,在下面便条的空缺处填上适当的内容。
According to the templet of example structure provided, fill in the correct terms in the following blanks.

_____条

_____:
　　今天上午____点,我来_____找您商谈有关_____事宜,不巧您正好_____不在,下午____点我再来,请您在_____等我。

　　　　_____

　　　　　　　　　　　　　　　　　　　　　　　　　_____
　　　　　　　　　　　　　　　　　　　　　　_____年___月___日

2 病例诊断
Case of illness diagnosis

根据上面所学的便条的知识,分析下面的例文在格式和措词上存在的毛病。
According to the note above, analyze the format and wording mistakes in the following example.

病例一
Case 1

请假条
朱老师:
　　我昨天感冒发烧,今天不能到校学习,今天感觉身体很不舒适,你必须要准假两天。
　　此致
　　敬礼

学生　王晶晶

二〇〇九年七月九日

病例二
Case 2

留言条

　　李经理，

　　今天上午九点，我来办公室找你商洽关于我爱人的工作调动问题，你外出了，不知干什么去了，害得我等了你一上午。你务必在明天等我，禁止外出。

此致

敬礼

刘　涛

2009年1月23日

3. 诊断结论
Diagnostic conclusion

根据你对练习 2 中两个病例的分析，按正确的写法写出来。

According to your analysis of the two cases, write out the right way of writing a note.

第二课 请 柬
Invitation

Basic principles and aims
要点提示

1. 了解请柬的基本用途、写作格式。
   Understand the basic purpose and writing formats of invitations.
2. 掌握请柬写作中语言、措词的基本特点。
   Master the basic characteristics of language and wording in invitation writing.
3. 基本掌握请柬的写法。
   Master the basics of invitation writing.

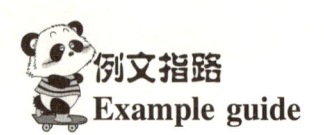

例文指路 Example guide

例文一
Example I

请柬①

刘诗涛教授：②

  谨订于1月12日下午6时在锦绣山庄二楼稻香阁雅厅为王学嘉教授饯行。③

  恭请

光临④

      李敬明⑤敬约⑥

写法注释
Writing notes

① **用途**：邀请机关、团体或个人参加某种活动、会议、聚会等时要写请柬，以示尊重、礼貌。"请柬"也可以写成"请帖"等字样。

② **称谓**：写明被邀请的单位名称或被请人的姓名。可在姓名后加上职称或先生、女士等称呼。

③ **正文**："谨订于"叫做启事语，也

2010年1月8日⑦

地址：育才街18号⑧

Invitation

Professor Liu Shitao,

　　The pleasure of your company is requested at a farewell dinner for Professor Wang Xuejia, at Jinxiu Restaurant in the second floor VIP room Dao Xiang Ge, on the twelfth of January at six o'clock in the evening.

　　We hope to be honoured by your presence.

Sincerely yours,
Li Jingming
January 8th, 2010

Address: No. 18 Yucai Street

可以写成"兹订于"、"拟于"、"订于"等。接下来要写明时间、地点、活动名称、内容等。

④ **邀请语**：有多种写法，如"敬请参加"、"敬请届时光临"、"恭候光临"等敬语。

⑤ **署名**：可以是发出邀请的单位的名称，或发出邀请的人的姓名，不可省略。

⑥ **文末敬语**：还可以写成"谨约"、"恳请"等。

⑦ **日期**：要写明发出邀请时的日期，年月日要写齐全。

⑧ **附启语**：地址等需要附带说明的内容，也可以省略。

① Purpose: When you invite a department, group, or individual to attend an activity, meeting, party etc., you should write them an invitation to show respect and politeness. 请柬 can also be expressed as 请帖 etc.

② Appellation: Clearly write the name of the company or person who is being invited. If the invitee is an individual, Mr., Mrs., Ms. etc. may all be used.

③ Text: 谨订于 are called beginning words, 兹订于, 拟于, 订于 etc. are also beginning words. Use these at the very start of the text, and then go on to describe the time, place, name of the activity etc.

④ Words of invitation: There are many terms that can be used to invite people, such as 敬请参加, 敬请届时光临, 恭候光临 etc.

⑤ Signature: The signature is a necessary part of the invitation, and can be the name of the company or of the individual who sent the invitation.

⑥ Honorific at the end of the invitation: This can be expressed as 谨约, 恳请 etc.

⑦ Date: The date of the invitation should be written fully, including the year, month and day.

⑧ Adjunction words: Added explanations such as the address and they can be omitted.

例文二
Example II

××电视台：①

兹订于五月四日晚八时整，在××大学礼堂举行『五四』青年诗歌朗诵会，届时恭请贵台记者光临。②

××大学团委会③

二〇〇九年五月二日④

写法注释
Writing notes

① 称谓：写明被邀请单位的名称或被请人的姓名。被邀请单位要写全称。如果邀请个人，可在姓名后加上职称或先生、女士等称呼。

② 正文："兹订于"叫做启事语，也可以写成"谨定于"、"拟订于"、"订于"等。接下来要写明时间、地点、活动名称、内容等。

③ 署名：发出邀请的单位的名称。如果是个人发出邀请，要写明姓名的全名，不可省略。

④ 日期：要写明发出邀请的日期，年月日要写齐全。

① Appellation: Clearly write the name of the company or person that is being invited. If the invitee is a company, the full name should be used. If the invitee is an individual, Mr., Mrs., Ms. etc. may all be used.

② Text: 兹订于 are called beginning words, 谨订于, 拟定于, 订于 etc. are also beginning words. Use these at the very start of the text, and then go on to describe the time, place, name of the activity etc.

③ Signature: The signature is a necessary part of the invitation, and can be the name of the company or of the individual who sent the invitation.

④ Date: The date of the invitation

第二课 请柬

XX TV Station:

Request the pleasure of you at a poetry declamation for the May 4th Youth Day, at the XX university auditorium on fourth of May at eight o'clock in the evening. Request the honour of the presence of your journalist.

XX University Communist Youth League
May 2nd, 2009

should be written fully, including the year, month and day.

生词 New words

请柬	qǐngjiǎn	invitation
教授	jiàoshòu	professor
锦绣	jǐnxiù	splendid
饯行	jiànxíng	give a farewell dinner
光临	guānglín	presence
礼堂	lǐtáng	auditorium
朗诵	lǎngsòng	recitation

结构模板 The template of structure

（一）横式结构
Pattern Structure

请柬①

□□□□□:②

　　谨订于(兹订于、拟于)□月□日□时在□□□□□□□举行(举办)□□□□□□□□□。③

　　恭请

光临④

　　　　　　　　　　　　　　　　　　　　□□□⑤ □□⑥

　　　　　　　　　　　　　　　　　　　　□□□□年□□月□□日⑦

　　□□□□□□□□⑧

模板格式说明

The template format explanation

① 标题:写明"请柬"字样,位置居中。通常写在请柬卡片的封面。

Caption: 请柬 should be written in the centre of the line. It is usually written on the front of invitation cards.

② 称谓:被邀请者要顶格写,后面加冒号。

Appellation: Write the invitee's name without indenting, follow it with a colon.

③ 正文:在称呼的下行写正文,首行空两格。

Text: There should be two spaces between the left margin and the first line of the text, which is below the appellation.

④ 邀请语:正文之下"恭请"前要空两个格,"光临"在"恭请"之下,顶格写。

Invitation words: 恭请 should be written with two spaces before it, 光临 should be written on the line below 恭请 and should not be preceded by a space.

⑤ 署名:在邀请语下一行右方署名。

Signature: Sign underneath the body of the invitation, on the right hand side of the page.

⑥ 文末敬语:在署名之后的同一行,一般与署名空一格。

Honorific at the end: This appears after the signature on the same line, usually separated by a space.

⑦ 日期:在署名和文末敬语的下一行。

Date: This is written on the line beneath the signature and the honorific.

⑧ 附启语：在请柬的最下边，前面空两个格。也可以省略。

Adjunction words: These can be written on the bottom left hand side of the invitation, preceded by two spaces. They can also be omitted.

（二）纵式结构
Vertical structure

请柬①

谨订于（兹订于、拟于）□□月□□日在□□□□□□□□举行（或举办）□□□□□②

□□□□□□。③

恭请

光临④

□□□□□□□□⑧

□□□□⑤

□□⑥

□□□□年□□月□□日⑦

模板格式说明

The template format explanation

① 标题:写明"请柬"字样,位置居中。通常写在请柬卡片的封面。

Caption: 请柬 should be written in the centre of the line. It is usually written on the front of invitation cards.

② 称谓:被邀请者要顶上格写,下面加冒号。

Appellation: Write the invitee's name without indenting, follow it with a colon.

③ 正文:在称谓的左边写正文,首行空两格。

Text: The text should be written at the left side of appellation. And there should be two spaces between the top margin and the first line of the text.

④ 邀请语:正文左边"恭请"前要空四个格,"光临"在"恭请"左边一行,前面空两个格。

Invitation words: 恭请 should be preceded on the left hand side of the text by four spaces from the top, 光临 should be written to the left of 恭请, and there should be two spaces from the top.

⑤ 署名:在邀请语左边一行下方署名。

Signature: The signature should be written below the invitation words on the left.

⑥ 文末敬语:在署名之下,一般与署名空一格。

Honorific at the end: This is written below the signature, with a space in between.

⑦ 日期:在署名和文末敬语的左边一行下方。

Date: This is written to the left of the signature and honorific.

⑧ 附启语:在请柬的最左边,前面空两个格。也可以省略。

Adjunction words: These can be written on the bottom left hand side of the invitation, preceded by two spaces. They can also be omitted.

第二课 请柬

1 照猫画虎
Follow the model

按照上面提示的结构模板,在下面请柬空缺处填上适当的内容。

According to the templet of structure provided, fill in the words in the following blanks.

_____
_____:
　　兹订于___月___日上午___点,在_____举办_____
_____。

　　　　　　　　　　　　　　　　　　　　　　　___年___月___日
_____

2 病例诊断
Case of illness diagnosis

根据上面所学的请柬的知识,分析下面的例文在格式和内容措词上存在的毛病。

According to the invitation above, analyze the format and content wording mistakes in the following example.

病　例
Case

请　柬

徐静女士：

　　兹订于3月15日晚上6时在新世纪演播大厅举办"3·15质量万里行"特别节

目，你务必准时参加。
恭请
　　　　　光临
地址：维新街23号

2009年3月12日
敬约　王主任

3 诊断结论
Diagnostic conclusion

请根据你对2题病例的分析，按结构模板的纵式结构用正确的写法写出来。
According to your analysis of the case above, write out the right way of writing an invitation.

第三课 日记
Diary

Basic principles and aims
要点提示

1. 了解日记的基本类型。
   Understand the basic types of diaries.
2. 掌握日记写作的格式。
   Master the format of diary writing.
3. 基本掌握日记的写法。
   Master the basics of diary writing.

例文一
Example I

鲁迅1932年10月15日日记①

十五日②　　　　　　　　晴③

上午给母亲寄了信。寄信的同时邮寄了《朝花夕拾》《三闲集》各一本。同广平带海婴到篠崎医院看病,付费十六元六角。把新版的K·Kollwitz画贴赠送给了坪井学士。收到大江书店的版税七十一元一角。晚上

写法注释
Writing notes

① **日记分类**：日记是常用的一种应用文体,是将一天中所见、所闻、所思、所感中重要的有价值的内容记录下来。日记按写作时使用的表达方式不同可以分为记叙类、议论类、描写类、抒情类、说明类和综合类六种类型。

② **日期**：完整的日期要写清年月日

邀请三弟全家来家吃螃蟹并一起吃晚饭。晚上有些胃痛。④

Lu Xun's Diary of October 15th, 1932

15th   Sunny

I sent a letter to mother in the morning, and also my two books 朝花夕拾 (*Morning Flowers Plucked at Dusk*) and 三闲集 (*Three Leisures*). Guangping and I carried Haiying to the Kozaki Hospital, and paid 16 *yuan* and 6 *jiao*. I gave the new edition of K. Kollwitz's Paintings to the scholar Tsuboi as a gift. I received 71 *yuan* and one *jiao* from Oe Bookstore for the royalty on my books. In the evening I invited my third youngest brother's family to come and have crabs for dinner. I had a stomachache at night.

和星期几,也可以只写月日。

③ **天气**:日记通常要写明天气情况。

④ **正文**:这是一则叙事类型的日记。每一句话记述一件事。语言简明扼要。日记正文语言一般要求口语化,而且行文要简洁。

① Diary types: A diary is a practical written account of the things one sees, hears, thinks and feels in a day. Diaries can be divided into six types: narrative, disputative, descriptive, expressive, expositive and comprehensive.

② Date: The date should include the year, month, date as well as the day of the week. It can also be written as the month and day.

③ Weather: The state of the weather is usually written in a diary.

④ Text: This is a narrative diary. Every sentence narrates an event. The language is simple and brief, and written in a colloquial style.

例文二
Example II

张海迪1981年7月7日日记①

1981年7月7日②

近来很多同志对我说希望我能参加个考试，弄到一张"文凭"。我考虑过，也向往得到一张文凭，我只是想用它来证明自己的学习成绩，而不想依仗它为自己谋取什么。说实话，我如果想得到这些，我可以辞掉所有的病号，谢绝所有的朋友，不再为他们的幸福和快乐费神；也许我可以埋在书堆里一个阶段。到时经过努力也许我真会得到一张盖着红印的文凭。但我不明白，那是否会帮助我多为人们做点什么。为了自己去忙碌总是没有什么意思的。那是自私的快乐和满足。记得马克思说过，能使大多数人幸福的人，他自己本身也是幸福的。我想做这样的人。③

Zhang Haidi's Diary of July 7th, 1981

July 7th, 1981

Recently many comrades have told me that they wish that I could sit an examination, and get a "diploma". I have considered it, and I look forward to getting one, but I only wish to have it as a record of my scholastic achievements. I do

写法注释
Writing notes

① 作者简介：张海迪(1955—)，女，山东文登人，青年作家。自幼患脊髓血管炎，高位截瘫。她以残疾之身，强忍病痛，从事创作，自学医学，并为别人解除病痛，表现出崇高的精神境界，成为中国青年学习的楷模。

② 日期：这则日记是年月日完整的日期形式，省略了星期几。(日期后省略了天气情况。)

③ 正文：这是一则议论型的日记。针对是否考文凭一事展开了议论。行文简洁，议论层次清楚。在文尾引用马克思的话，使这一事件的意义得到了提升。

① Introduction to the author: Zhang Haidi (1955–), female, is a young writer who was born in Wendeng, Shandong Province. She has suffered from spinal cord vasculitis since childhood, and has paraplegia. She engaged to study medicine by herself, and has gone on to treat other disabled patients, helping to relieve their symptoms and reduce their serious illnesses. She has high and optimistic spirits, and is a model for Chinese youth to study.

② Date: This diary shows the year, month and date, but omits what day of the week the entry was not wish to depend on it to get things. To be honest, if I just wanted to acquire things I could decline all patients, refuse all friends and not trouble myself with their happiness. Maybe I can shut myself up among books for a period. Maybe I really can get a diploma with a red seal through my own efforts. I am just not sure that that will help me to do more for people. It seems meaningless to be busy on one's own business. It is selfish joy and satisfaction. I remember that Marx said that someone who can give the greatest number of people happiness is the one who will achieve the greatest happiness. I want to be such a person.

written on. It also does not mention the weather conditions of the day.

③ Text: This is a disputative diary. It disputes whether or not she should take an examination for a diploma. It is written and arranged in a clear and simple style. Her quoting of Marx takes the subject to a higher level.

 生 词
New words

日记	rìjì	diary
付费	fùfèi	pay
文凭	wénpíng	diploma
谋取	móuqǔ	get
病号	bìnghào	patient
谢绝	xièjué	refuse
费神	fèishén	trouble

第三课 日记

结构模板
The template of structure

□□□□年□□月□□日①　星期□②　　　　　　　　　□□③
　　□□□□□□□□□□□□□□□□□□□□□□□
□□□□□□□□□□□□□。④

模板格式说明

The template format explanation

① 日期：第一行先写明完整的日期，要写清年月日，有时也可以只写月日。

Date: Write the complete date, including year, month, day. Sometimes only write month and day.

② 星期：位于日期之后空一格。

what day: Take a space after the date.

③ 天气：在星期之后空一格写明天气情况。

Weather: Take a space after the week.

④ 正文：第二行开始写正文。首行空两格。

Text: Write the text from the second line. Take two spaces in the first line.

练习
Exercises

1 例文评析
Example analysis

按照上面提示的日记的格式及写法，分析下面这则日记的类型及写作格式和语言上的优点。

According to the diary's format and way of writing provided, analyze the type and characteristics of the writing format and language in the following diary entry.

21

10月25日　　星期六　　晴

今天,我参观了东方明珠电视塔,它是上海的新象征。

东方明珠电视塔高达468米——位居亚洲第二,世界第四,重量为125000吨。

东方明珠电视塔能帮助传送广播和电视节目,塔内有6架高速电梯,人们上到电梯里,可以欣赏上海的美景。

塔内有11个钢"球",它们看起来就像天窗中11颗美丽的珍珠。最高的一个被称为"太空屋",它有350米高。从"太空屋"上去,可以到达塔顶,它的高度为468米。如果你想在塔里过夜,那里有宾馆、KTV包间和迪斯科舞厅供你选择。

2 照猫画虎
Follow the model

按照上面提示的例文结构模板写一则日记。

According to the templet of example structure provided, write a diary entry.

第四课 启 事
Notice

Basic principles and aims
要点提示

1. 了解启事的常见类型。
   Understand the common types of notices.
2. 掌握常见启事的写作格式和语言特点。
   Master the writing format and language characteristics of common notices.
3. 基本掌握常见启事的写法。
   Master the basics of notice writing.

例文指路
Example guide

例文一
Example I

寻物启事①

本人于6月3日(星期一)下午5时许,在15路公共汽车上不慎遗失黑色牛皮公文包一个。有仁人君子拾获者,请将包内的身份证和经济合同寄"舞阳新屯3栋6号吴立功"收;或打电话4367531找吴先生。皮包及其余钱物愿移以为赠。万分感激!②

失主 吴立功③

写法注释
Writing notes

① 标题类型:向社会或某个(些)人公开发布某一信息时使用启事。这篇例文是一则常见的寻物启事。

② 正文:寻物启事的正文要写明何时、何地、丢失东西的原因及遗失物的显著特征,还要写明拾到者如何与失主联系、表示感谢等内容。

23

Lost

On June 3rd (Monday) at around five o'clock in the afternoon, on bus No. 15, a black cowhide briefcase was lost. If found, please return the ID card and the economic contract in the briefcase by post to "Wu Ligong, No. 6 Building 3, Wuyang Xintun". The briefcase itself, the money and other contents are offered as a reward for the return of these two items. Or please call Mr. Wu on 4367531. Thank you.

Wu Ligong

③ 署名：一般要写明失主的姓名。

① Caption types: Notices are used when releasing information to the general public, or someone specific. This is an example of a notice informing people of the loss of an item.

② Text: The text for this type of notice should include when and where the item was lost, the reason for its loss, and the recognisable characteristics of the lost item. It should also include the way for the finder of the item to contact its owner, and express gratitude to the finder.

③ Signature: Clearly write the name of the owner of the lost item.

例文二
Example II

文慧中学校庆活动启事①

今年10月15日是本校八十周年校庆，届时将举办各项庆祝活动。兹订于15日上午9时在本校人文科学馆的学术报告厅举行纪念大会，并在该馆南厅举办本校八十周年建校成就展览。热烈欢迎各届校友返校参观指导，共商本校发展大计。②

联系地址：湖北省十堰市车城西路94号文慧中学校庆办公室

邮编：442003

联系人：王老师、李老师

联系电话：0719-84023833

传真：0719-83092930

网址：http://www.wxzhx.edu.cn

电子邮件：xpwyh@wxzhx.edu.cn③

欢迎各位校友届时返校同庆！④

文慧中学校庆筹备委员会⑤

写法注释
Writing notes

① 标题类型：这是一则活动启事。这则启事的标题写明了活动的具体名称。

② 正文：要写明活动的原因、目的及时间、地点，举办活动的名称、具体内容、希望哪些人参加等。

③ 联系方式：一般要写明活动的联系地址、电话、联系人等。

④ 补充事项：有另外需要补充说明的事项可以在补充事项部分写明。

⑤ 署名：一般要写明活动主办单位的全称。

① Caption types: This is a notice announcing an activity. The caption states the name of the activity.

② Text: This should include the reason, purpose, time, place, name, expected participants and an outline of the activity.

③ Contact information: This should clearly include the name, telephone number, address etc. of the contact person for the activity.

④ Supplement: If there is added information that needs to be included, it should be written in this section.

⑤ Signature: The full name of the activity organiser or sponsor should be written.

Notice of Wenhui High School's Anniversary Celebrations

This year we celebrate our school's eightieth anniversary on October 15th, when we shall begin to hold various celebratory activities. There is a commemorate conference to be held on the 15th at 9 a.m. in the Academic Report Hall, which is located in the Literary Humanities Building in the school. There will also be an exhibition of the school's achievements over the past eighty years held in the Southern Hall of the same building. We wish to extend a warm welcome to alumni to return to participate in, guide and discuss the plans for our school.

Address: Wenhui High School Anniversary Celebration Office

No. 94 Checheng West Road

Shiyan, Hubei Province

442003

Contact: Mr. Wang, Mr. Li

Tel: 0719-84023833

Fax: 0719-83092930

Website: http://www.wxzhx.edu.cn

E-mail: xpwyh@wxzhx.edu.cn

We welcome the return of past students to the school for our celebration!

The Anniversary Celebration Preparatory Committee

Wenhui High School

例文三
Example Ⅲ

夏安证券公司征聘启事①

夏安证券公司现征聘电脑管理员2名,具体要求如下:

男女不限,年龄在40岁以下;计算机专业本科以上学历;掌握局域网管理与计算机通讯技术,有较强的编程能力;身体健康,敬业精神强。有证券从业经验者优先。

有意者请于7月30日前将个人身份证、学历证书的复印件及简历一份、2寸近照一张寄至我公司。②

通信地址:北京东路81号国宾大厦3楼夏安证券公司办公室,邮编100090

联系电话:88109889

联系人:刘女士、陈先生③

谢绝来访④

A Xia'an Securities Company Job Advertisement

Xia'an Securities Company is currently looking for two computer administrators who meet the following requirements:

Male or female, under 40 years old, with an undergraduate degree or above in computer science, who master LAN management and

写法注释
Writing notes

① **标题类型**:这是一则征聘类启事。这类启事的标题可以写成"征(招)聘启事",也可以像例文一样在征聘启事前写明招聘单位的名称。

② **正文**:要写明征聘人员的条件要求,包括性别、年龄、学历、专业、有无工作经验等内容。

③ **联系方式**:一般要写明招聘单位地址、联系电话、联系人等内容。

④ **补充事项**:如有提请受聘者注意的其他事项,可以在文末补充事项中写明。

① Caption types: This is a job advertisement. This notice can have its caption written as 征(招)聘启事, or can use the name of the company before it as is seen in this example.

② Text: This should include the requirements for the job, including age, sex, education and work experience etc.

③ Contact information: The name, telephone number, address etc. of the company contact person should be clearly written.

④ Supplement: If there is added information that needs to be included, it should be written in this section.

computer communication technology. Ability to program at a high level, and a healthy and energetic professional attitude. Previous experience working in securities is preferred.

Applicants need to send a copy of their ID cards, educational qualifications, a resume and a two-inch photo to our company before July 30th.

Address: Xia'an Securities Company Office Building 3, Guobin Building No. 81 Beijing East Road

Zip code: 100090

Tel: 88109889

Contact: Ms. Liu, Mr. Chen

Applicants may only apply via post.

生 词
New words

启事	qǐshì	notice
遗失	yíshī	lose
君子	jūnzǐ	man of honour
校庆	xiàoqìng	school's anniversary celebration
校友	xiàoyǒu	schoolfellow / alumnus
筹备	chóubèi	preparatory
征聘	zhēngpìn	invite applications for jobs
敬业精神	jìngyè jīngshén	professional dedication

结构模板
The template of structure

□□启事①

□□□□□□□□□□□□□□□□□□□□□□□□□□□□□□□□□。②

通信地址：□□□□□□□□

联系电话：□□□□□□□□
联系人：□□□③
　　□□□□□□□□□□。④

　　　　　　　　　　　　　　　　　□□□□
　　　　　　　　　　　　　　　　□□□□□⑤

模板格式说明

The template format explanation

① 标题类型：写明启事类型名称，位置居中。

Caption types: The name and type of the notice should be centred on the page.

② 正文：根据不同类型的启事的写作要求，在标题下行写正文，每段段首要空两格。

Text: According to the needs of different notices, write on the next line down, and indent all new paragraphs.

③ 联系方式：在正文之下要写明联系方式，例如联系人、联系电话、通信地址等。每项前空两格。

Contact information: Write out the contact information, such as the contact person's name, telephone number, address etc. clearly below the text. Each item should be preceded by two spaces.

④ 补充事项：在联系方式之下、署名前，补充事项前要空两格。

Supplement: This should be written below the contact information, and above the signature, with two spaces indented.

⑤ 署名：在正文右下角要写明启事发出者的姓名或单位名称。

Signature: The author or company's name should be clearly written below the text in the bottom right hand corner.

1. 顺藤摘瓜
Track by following clues

寻人启事与寻物启事同属一类,写法相似,请按照例文一和结构模板提示,写一则寻人启事。

The notice of lost someone and the notice of lost something are the same kind, they have similar writing way. According to example one and the templet of structure please write a notice of lost someone.

2. 照猫画虎
Follow the model

按照例文三的结构特点,将下面的"征文启事"补充完整。

According to the structural characteristics of example 3, complete the following "Notice of Contributions Wanted".

纪念世界反法西斯胜利六十五周年"和平杯"征文启事

为纪念世界反法西斯胜利六十五周年,中国写作学会特举办以"我们爱和平"为主题的征文活动。具体要求如下:

(1) 奖励办法:＿＿＿＿＿＿＿＿＿＿
(2) 起止时间:＿＿＿＿＿＿＿＿＿＿
(3) 文体要求:＿＿＿＿＿＿＿＿＿＿
(4) 作品字数:＿＿＿＿＿＿＿＿＿＿

通信地址:＿＿＿＿＿＿＿＿＿＿
邮政编码:＿＿＿＿＿＿＿＿＿＿
联系电话:＿＿＿＿＿＿＿＿＿＿
联 系 人:＿＿＿＿＿＿＿＿＿＿
电子邮件:＿＿＿＿＿＿＿＿＿＿
注意事项:＿＿＿＿＿＿＿＿＿＿

第五课 介绍信
Letter of Introduction

Basic principles and aims
要点提示

1. 了解介绍信的用途。
   Understand the purpose of letters of introduction.
2. 掌握介绍信的写作格式和语言特点。
   Master the writing format and language characteristics of letters of introduction.
3. 基本掌握介绍信的写法。
   Master the basics of writing a letter of introduction.

例文指路
Example guide

例文
Example

介 绍 信①

春季服装产品展销中心：②

  兹介绍我公司销售部经理崔向民和副经理霍俊峰前往贵处联系我公司服装产品参展事宜，请予接洽，并给予支持协助为盼。③

  此致
敬礼④

写法注释
Writing notes

① 用途：适用于国家行政机关、企事业单位联系工作、了解情况等时所用的一种印刷文件。具有证明和介绍的双重作用，有固定格式。一般有编号和存根，以备日后查询。

② 称谓：写明收信单位的全称。

③ 正文：要写明被介绍人的姓名、职务，前往的目的及要办理事务的内容，并在文末附有"请予接

新时尚服装有限公司

2010年1月4日 ⑤

Letter of Introduction

The Sales Exhibition Centre of Spring Clothing Products:

  We wish to introduce Cui Xiangmin and Huo Junfeng, our company's sales manager and assistant manager. They are in charge of co-ordinating our clothing products that are to be shown in the exhibition. Please inform them of any arrangements that need to be made. We are looking forward to your support and assistance.

  Best Wishes!

New Fashion Clothing Ltd.
January 4th, 2010

洽"、"请予办理"、"请给予协助为盼"等希望性敬语。

④ **文末敬语**：一般使用"此致,敬礼"等敬语。

⑤ **署名**：写明发出介绍信的单位名称和时间,并要盖章。

① Purpose: A printed document used in government administrations, enterprises and state owned institutions, between people to introduce and make contacts. It has a fixed format, and usually includes a serial number and receipt stub for reference if there are further inquiries.

② Appellation: Write the full name of the recipient of the letter without indenting.

③ Text: Write the full name of the person being introduced, the purpose for their visit, the main outlines of the matter at hand, and make sure to add an honorific phrase such as 请予接洽, 请予办理, 请给予协助为盼 etc. to the end of the text.

④ Honorific at the end: Such an honorific as 此致, 敬礼 etc. are usually used for these kinds of letters.

⑤ Signature: Write the full name of the author or organisation that is issuing the letter, followed by the date and time of its creation and it should be sealed.

第五课 介绍信

生词
New words

展销	zhǎnxiāo	sales exhibition
销售部	xiāoshòubù	sales department
接洽	jiēqià	arrange
协助	xiézhù	assist

结构模板
The template of structure

介绍信①

□□□□：②

　　□□。③

　此致

敬礼④

　　　　　　　　　　　　　　　　　　□□□□□□

　　　　　　　　　　　　　　　　　　□□□□年□□月□□日⑤

模板格式说明

The template format explanation

① 标题："介绍信"位置要居中。

Caption: The heading should be centred on the page.

② 称谓：收信单位的全称要顶格写，后面加冒号。

Appellation: Write the full name of the recipient of the letter without indenting, followed by a colon.

③ 正文：要写明被介绍人的姓名、职务、前往的目的及要办理事务的内容，并在文末使用"请予接洽"、"请予办理"、"请给予协助为盼"等希望性敬语。

Text: Write the full name of the person being introduced, the purpose for their visit, the

33

main outlines of the matter at hand, and make sure to add an honorific phrase such as 请予接洽, 请予办理, 请予以协助为盼 etc. to the end of the text.

④ 文末敬语:"此致"在正文下一行,前面空两格,"敬礼"在"此致"下一行,顶格写。

Honorific at the end: Such an honorific as 此致, 敬礼 etc. are usually used for these kinds of letters.

⑤ 署名:在敬语右下方写明发信单位或个人名称和发信时间。

Signature: Write the full name of the author or organisation that is issuing the letter, followed by the date and time of its creation.

练习 Exercises

1 照猫画虎 Follow the model

按照例文和结构模板的提示,将下面的"介绍信"补充完整。
According to the example and the template of structure, complete the following "Letter of Introduction"

介绍信

_____:

  兹介绍我单位_____和_____两位同志前往贵单位商洽_____事宜,敬请_____。

2 顺藤摘瓜 Follow the clues

请根据例文写法注释和结构模板写法提示,自拟一则介绍信。
Following the example note and the template of structure, write a letter of introduction.

第六课 求职信
Letter of Application

Basic principles and aims
要点提示

1. 了解求职信的格式和语言特点。
   Understand the format of letters of application and their language characteristics.
2. 基本掌握求职信的写法。
   Master the basics of writing letters of application.

例文指路
Example guide

例文
Example

求职信①

尊敬的领导：②

　　您好！③

　　首先感谢您在百忙之中抽出时间阅读我的自荐书，希望这是我施展才华、实现自我价值的一个良好开端。

　　我是英语专业的学生，欣闻贵公司正需要我们这类人才的加盟，贵公司雄厚的实力和蒸蒸日上的发展前景深深吸引着

写法注释
Writing notes

① 用途：又名自荐书、自荐信等，是求职者向用人单位负责人呈递的一种专门书信。

② 称谓：一般写为"尊敬的领导"，也可以写成"尊敬的主管"等。

③ 问候语：常见的问候语是"您好！"，也可以写成"您好，您工作辛苦了！"等等，不拘一格。

④ 正文：求职者的自我简介，主要包括所学专业、思想、社会实践等情况，要突出自己的优点或专

我。更素闻贵公司重视人才,爱才如宝,因此,我希望能够加入到这个团体中,为公司的发展增砖添瓦,尽我的一份力量。古语云:"世有伯乐,而后有千里马。"我不敢自认是千里马,但争做千里马的决心和信心一直鼓满心胸。我相信,给我一个能够发挥的舞台,我必能以出色的业绩来证明自己。

　　随信附上简历和其他材料一份。如需更深了解,请给我一次面试的机会!④

　　最后祝您工作顺利!
　　此致
敬礼⑤

求职人　陈莉莉
2009年4月23日⑥

长,表达出求职者的信心和愿望等。语言既要言简意赅,讲究一定的文采,又要有说服力,还要注意语气谦和,多用敬语。

⑤ **文末敬语**:一般使用"此致,敬礼",也可以在此之前加上"祝您工作顺利,身体健康"等敬语。

⑥ **署名**:写明求职人的姓名及时间。

① Caption: This is also known as a cover letter. It is a letter that is presented to potential employers.

② Appellation: The letter usually begins with the term 尊敬的领导 or 尊敬的主管 etc.

③ Greeting: Commonly used greetings are 您好, 您工作辛苦了 and so on. Greetings are not limited to a specific type; many different types can be used.

④ Text: This is where the applicant introduces themselves, and can describe their relevant education history, social skills, and ideologies. It should focus on their special skills and talents, and express the job seeker's confidence in their ability to perform the job. The language should be clear and concise, with care taken to use correct language grammar. The tone should be modest and polite.

⑤ Honorific at the end: 此致, 敬礼 are usually used, and often 祝您工作顺利 and 身体健康 etc. are added before them as well.

⑥ Signature: The job seeker's name, and the date of the letter's creation should both be written clearly.

Letter of Application

Dear Sir/Madam:

Hello, first allow me to thank you for taking time out of your busy schedule to read my application. I hope this is a good sign of things to come, as I believe I possess the knowledge and ability to actualise my personal worth that will allow me to perform this job successfully.

I am an English major, so it was with happiness that I heard that your company was looking for additional workers to join your team. The tremendous existing strength of your company and its wonderful future prospects attract me. Your reputation for valuing talent and nurturing it increases my wish to join your group and contribute to its success and development. There is a Chinese saying: "Even if you are talented, you need an opportunity to succeed", I would not presume to call myself amazingly talented, but I possess determination and confidence in my abilities. I believe that if given the opportunity, I will be able to prove myself through my achievements.

I have enclosed my resume and related references with this letter, if there is anything more you wish to know I will be more than happy to come in for an interview.

All the best with your work!
Many thanks.

Sincerely,
Chen Lili
April 23rd, 2009

生词
New words

施展	shīzhǎn	exhibit
加盟	jiāméng	join
蒸蒸日上	zhēngzhēng rì shàng	prosper with each passing day
增砖添瓦	zēng zhuān tiān wǎ	make great efforts
伯乐	Bólè	talent scout
业绩	yèjì	achievement

结构模板
The template of structure

求职信①

尊敬的□□:②

　　您好!③

　　□□□□□□□□□□□□□□□□□□□□□□□□□□□。

　　□□□□□□□□□□□□□□□□□□□□□□□□□□□□

　　□□□□□□□□□□□□□□□□□□□□□□□□□。④

　　最后祝您□□□□□□!

　　此致

敬礼⑤

求职人□□□
□□□□年□□月□□日⑥

模板格式说明

The template format explanation

① 标题:位置要居中。

Caption: This should be centred on the page.

② 称谓:标题下第一行顶格写。

Appellation: Written on the line below the caption without indenting.

③ 问候语:称谓之下,前空两格。

Greeting: Written below the appellation with two spaces preceding it.

④ 正文:段首空两格。行文中注意分清层次段落。

Text: The first line should be preceded by two spaces. Paragraphs should be arranged clearly.

⑤ 文末敬语:"此致"前要空两格,"敬礼"在此致下行顶格写。

Honorific at the end: 此致 should be preceded by two spaces. 敬礼 is written unindented on the line directly below 此致.

⑥ 署名:信的右下方,求职人姓名在上,日期在下。

Signature: This should be written at the bottom right hand side of the page, beneath the text. The date should be written below the applicant's name.

练习 Exercises

1 例文评析
Example analysis

下面是一则规范的求职信,请根据自己所学的求职信的写作知识,对下面这份求职信的格式、内容、语言等方面进行评析。

The following is a letter of application, according to what you have learned about writing letters of application, analyze the following letter of application's format, content, language, etc.

求职信

尊敬的领导：

  您好！

  我是一名xx专业的毕业生。非常感谢您在百忙之中抽出时间，阅读我这份自荐材料，给我一次迈向成功的机会。

  大学四年转眼即过，我满怀希望地走进社会这个更加博大的课堂。当今世界充满竞争，充满挑战，也充满了机遇。我希望能从贵公司得到一个机遇、一个舞台，用我所学去服务公司，服务社会。

  大学期间，本着严谨求学的态度，在学习中我注重实践能力的培养，把专业知识与实践相结合，积极主动地参加各种社会活动，将我所学用于实践，不断增强自己的工作能力，为今后开展各项工作打下坚实的基础。在英语方面，我通过了国家英语四、六级考试，具备良好的听、说、写、译的能力。在计算机方面，我广泛地学习了计算机软、硬件方面的知识，能熟练地运用Windows2000/xp、Office等软件，并通过了国家计算机二级考试，同时对Internet有一定的了解，能够有效地利用互联网资源。

  怀着自信我向您推荐自己，如果有幸成为贵公司的一员，我愿从小事做起，从现在做起，虚心尽责、勤奋工作，在实践中不断学习，发挥自己的主动性、创造性，竭力为公司的发展添一份光彩。

  最后，再次感谢您阅读此信，期待着您的早日答复。愿贵单位兴旺发达！

  此致

敬礼

王新涛 敬呈
2009年12月11日

2 照猫画虎
Follow the model

按照例文和结构模板的提示，为自己写一份求职信。

According to the example and the template of structure, write a letter of application for yourself.

第七课　申请书
Application

Basic principles and aims
要点提示

1. 了解申请书的格式和语言特点。
   Understand the format and language characteristics of applications.
2. 基本掌握申请书的写法。
   Master the basics of application writing.

例文指路
Example guide

例文
Example

入学申请书①

刊授大学尊敬的先生、女士：②

　　你们好！③

　　我是居住在英国伦敦的一名华人。我从一个在上海的朋友那里得知你们在国内举办"刊授大学"的消息，颇感兴趣，所以不惜隔着千山万水，写信申请。

　　我很小便跟随父母移居英国，每天在学校学习的当然是英文。但是我不能因居

写法注释
Writing notes

① **用途**：入学申请是向有关学校或单位提出申请，希望前往求学或进修学习时使用的一种书信体应用文。

② **称谓**：一般写为"尊敬的领导"，也可以写成"尊敬的学校负责人"等。

③ **问候语**：常见的问候语是"您好！"，也可以写成"您好，您工作辛苦了！"等等，不拘一格。

④ **正文**：正文是申请书的核心部

住在另一国家而忘记祖国的语言。试想,身为一个中国人而不懂自己国家的语言是一件多么羞耻的事!所以,我坚持不断地每星期六到伦敦开办的中文学校学习。由于多年来的刻苦学习,我的中文水平已大有提高。但是非常可惜,这所学校并没有设置较深的中文课程,所教的无非是些基础和补习性质的中文课,所以我只好在空闲的时间自修。我酷爱祖国悠久的文化、历史、语言,这促使我想深入学习并了解有关中国文学的各方面知识。但在英国,这个条件非常差,无法满足我强烈的愿望。现在,我的这位朋友跟我谈及了有关你们在国内举办的"刊授大学",我便请他设法替我申请。我已阅读了大量的中文书籍、刊物,中国的许多文学名著我都看过,我还每天阅读中文报纸。

在英国,虽然有无数的函授学校,但所授的大多是商业、科技等专业,文科的专业非常少,更不要说中国语言文学专业了。我知道我申请入学会带给先生、女士们很多麻烦,但我相信你们会谅解我求知心切,理解我多么希望能够跟随"刊授大学"学习的心情!你们若想从各个方面了解我,只要来信告知,我会尽我所能答复你们的一切问题。④

请接受我衷心的谢意!⑤

学生 周玉芬

2010年3月16日于伦敦⑥

分,主要写明申请入学的理由。正文中要讲明自己原来的一些学习经历或情况,还需将自己要在该校的学习打算及具体入校要求写出来,这样可以使学校恰当地安排你的专业及学习的级别。申请书的语言要求简明扼要,态度要诚恳,语气要谦和,措词要注意敬语的使用。就本篇例文来看,作者申请的目的、理由是明确而具体的,语言的准确运用显示了作者较好的文字功底。文章篇幅长短适中,对有些问题的询问方式态度谦和,兼顾礼仪,于轻松的行文中,让我们感到作者的真诚。

⑤ **文末敬语**:一般使用"此致,敬礼",也可以使用"祝您工作顺利,身体健康"等敬语。

⑥ **署名**:写明申请人的姓名及申请时间。

① Purpose: Applications for admission are used for applying to schools or organisations that one wishes to attend for study.

② Appellation: 尊敬的领导 and 尊敬的学校负责人 etc. are usually used.

③ Greeting: Commonly used greetings are 您好 or 您好,您工作辛苦了 and so on. Greetings are not limited to a specific type, many different types can be used.

④ Text: This is the core section in applications for admission, as it deals with the reasons for application. It should include previous study experiences and future study plans and specifications, so that the institute applied can arrange a major at an

Application for Admission

Dear Sir/Madame of the Correspondence University:

Hello.

I am a Chinese living abroad in London, England. I have heard from a friend in Shanghai of the Correspondence University that is run at home, and in which I have a great interest. So much in fact that thousands of mountains and rivers could not prevent me from writing an application to you.

I immigrated to England with parents as a young child, and of course have studied at school here in English. However, even though I live abroad I have never forgotten the language of my mother country. Try to imagine being Chinese, but being unable to understand your own country's language, how shameful! So, to avoid this I have been studying every Saturday at a Chinese school in London, and as a result of many years of assiduous study, my Chinese has greatly improved. However, unfortunately my

appropriate level. The language used should be clear and concise, using polite language and written in a modest tone. In this example the author's reasons for applying are clear and definite, and the composition demonstrates the author's written abilities. It is of moderate length and reflects the author's request, feelings and attitude accurately.

⑤ Honorific at the end: 此致，敬礼 and 祝您工作顺利，身体健康 etc. are usually used.

⑥ Signature: The applicant's name, and the date of the application's writing should both be written clearly.

school only offered courses in foundational and remedial Chinese, and did not cover more advanced Chinese, therefore I have needed to study more deeply in my spare time to advance my Chinese. I am very proud of my motherland's deep culture, history, and language, and these things encourage me to advance my studies and gain a wider knowledge of Chinese literature. However in England the conditions for learning about such things are not ideal, and I have been unable to sate my intense desire for such knowledge. Now however, I have heard about the Correspondence University in China, and I have asked my friend to help me apply for a place in your university. I have already read a large number of Chinese books, magazines, and many Chinese literary masterpieces, and I also read the Chinese newspapers every day.

In England, although there are many correspondence schools, they mostly specialise in business, science and technology, those focusing on the liberal arts are very few, and of course none offer courses in Chinese literature. I know that my application is likely to cause you much trouble, but I hope you will forgive me as my desire for knowledge and wish to study at the Correspondence University is so very serious and sincere! If there is anything else you wish to know, I would be more than happy to answer any and all questions.

With Sincere Thanks,

Zhou Yufen

March 16th, 2010 London

第七课 申请书

生词 New words

得知	dézhī	know
试想	shìxiǎng	try to imagine
羞耻	xiūchǐ	shame
补习	bǔxí	remediation
空闲	kòngxián	spare
酷爱	kù'ài	have a craze for
悠久	yōujiǔ	timehonored
谅解	liàngjiě	forgive
求知心切	qiúzhī xīnqiè	eager for knowledge
衷心	zhōngxīn	heartfelt

结构模板 The template of structure

申请书①

尊敬的□□:②

　　您好！③

　　□□□。④

　　最后祝您□□□□□□！⑤

　　　　　　　　　　　　　　　申请人□□□
　　　　　　　　　　　　□□□□年□□月□□日⑥

模板格式说明

The template format explanation

① 标题：位置要居中。

Caption: This should be centred on the page.

② 称谓：标题下第一行顶格写。

Appellation: Written on the line below the caption without indenting.

③ 问候语：称谓之下，前空两格。

Greeting: Written below the appellation with two spaces preceding it.

④ 正文：段首空两格。行文中注意分清层次段落。

Text: The first line should indent two spaces. Paragraphs should be arranged clearly.

⑤ 文末敬语：正文结束下一段，行首空两格。

Honorific at the end: This should be written on the line below the final line of the text. It should be preceded by two spaces.

⑥ 署名：信的右下方，求职人姓名在上，日期在下。

Signature: This should be written at the bottom right hand side of the page, beneath the text. The date should be written below the applicant's name.

练习 Exercises

1 顺藤摘瓜
Follow the clues

按照例文和结构模板的提示，根据下面提供的材料，写一份申请书。

According to the example and the templet of structure, write an application based on the following material.

材料：

　　xx学校08级会计二班的学生夏秋叶在去年的一次体育课上,由于不慎摔了一跤,造成了左腿骨折。经过一年的治疗和调养,现已基本痊愈,为了不耽误下学期的课程,现特提出申请,请求复学。在一年的休养过程中,她始终没有放松学习,还自学了这一年所落下的课程,请求在复学时可以跟原班学习,不要留级。

2 照猫画虎
Follow the model

按照例文的"写法注释"和结构模板的"格式说明",试着写一份入学申请书。
According to the writing notes in the example and the template structure explanation, try to write an application for admission.

第八课

贺 信
Letter of Congratulation

Basic principles and aims
要点提示

1. 了解贺信的用途。
   Understand the purpose of letters of congratulation.
2. 掌握贺信的格式和语言特点。
   Master the format and language characteristics of letters of congratulation.
3. 基本掌握贺信的写法。
   Master the basics of writing letters of congratulation.

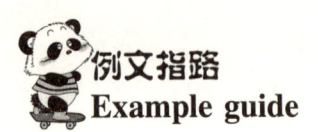

例文指路 Example guide

例文
Example

致惠特曼书 ①

亲爱的先生:②

  对于才华横溢的《草叶集》,我不是看不见它的价值的。我认为它是美国至今所能贡献的最了不起的聪明才智的菁华。我在读它的时候,感到十分愉快,伟大的力量总是使我们感到愉快的。我一向认

写法注释
Writing notes

① 用途:贺信是向个人、集体、团体或单位表示祝贺的一种书信。

② 称谓:贺信接受者,一般写为"尊敬的×××",或"亲爱的×××"等。

为，我们似乎处于贫脊枯竭的状态，好像过多的雕凿，或者过多的迂缓气质正把我们西方的智慧变得迟钝而平庸，《草叶集》正是我们所需要的。我为您的自由和勇敢的思想而高兴。我为它感到非常高兴。我发现美妙无比的事物，正像应该表现的那样，表现得无比美妙。我还发现那种大胆的处理，它使我们感到十分高兴，恐怕只有深刻的理解力，才能够启发它。

在一个伟大事业伊始之际，为了这样良好的开端，我恭贺您。这个开端将来一定会有广阔的前景。我揉揉眼睛，想看看这道阳光是不是幻觉；但是这本书给我的实感又是明确无疑的。它的最大优点就是加强和鼓舞人们的信心。

直到昨天晚上，我在一家报纸上看见本书的广告时，我才相信真有此书，而且能在邮局里买到。

我盼望和您这位良师益友能有机会见上一面，很想能撇下工作到纽约来拜访您。③

R·W·爱默生④
1855年7月21日
于马萨诸塞州康科德⑤

③ **正文**：正文是贺信的核心部分，要写明因何事表示祝贺，祝贺的理由，对对方的成绩、贡献、帮助、事迹等等进行评价并表示祝贺。语言使用上体现出写信人的热烈祝贺的心情，所以语言热情洋溢，感情饱满，讲究措词和文采。本例文作者爱默生对惠特曼刚刚出版的作品给予了很高的评价，接着表达了对惠特曼的衷心祝贺，最后表达了能与作者会面的强烈愿望。语言简洁生动，用词准确，文采飞扬，感情充沛，恰到好处。

④ **作者简介**：爱默生(1803—1882)，美国哲学家、诗人、散文家。此信写于美国诗人惠特曼(1819—1892)的诗集《草叶集》刚刚出版之时。

⑤ **署名**：写明写信人的姓名，写信的时间及地点。

① Purpose: A letter of congratulation is a letter that expresses congratulations to an individual, collective, group or organisation.

② Appellation: The receiver is usually addressed as 'Honourable xxxx' or 'Dear xxxx' etc.

③ Text: This is the main section in letters of congratulation, as it details the reasons for congratulation, expresses praise and congratulations for the relevant achievements, contributions, deeds etc. The language used should reflect the sincerity of the writer's warm congra-tulations, and the wording should be accurate. In this example the author Emerson praises Whitman's latest work

Emerson's Letter to Whitman

Dear Sir:

  I am not blind to the worth of the wonderful gift of *Leaves of Grass*. I find it the most extraordinary piece of wit and wisdom that America has yet contributed. I am very happy in reading it, as great power makes us happy. It meets the demand I am always making of what seemed the sterile and stingy nature, as if too much handiwork, or too much lymph in the temperament, were making our western wits fat and mean. I give you joy of your free and brave thought. I have great joy in it. I find incomparable things said incomparably well, as they must be. I find the courage of treatment which so delights us, and which large perception only can inspire.

  I greet you at the beginning of a great career, which yet must have had a long foreground somewhere, for such a start. I rubbed my eyes a little, to see if this sunbeam were no illusion; but the solid sense of the book is a sober certainty. It has the best merits, namely, of fortifying and encouraging.

  I did not know until I last night saw the book advertised in newspaper that I could trust the name as real and available for a post-office.

  I wish to see my benefactor, and have felt much like striking my tasks, and visiting New York to pay you my respects.

R.W. Emerson
21st July, 1855
Concord, Massachusetts

very highly, before expressing his sincere thanks to Whitman. Finally he expresses a strong desire to meet with the author to deliver his respects in person. The language is clear and vivid, and clearly displays the author's literary talent, the sentiment is warm and the language is appropriate for this type of letter.

④ Introduction to the author: Emerson (1803 –1882), was an American philosopher, poet and essayist. At the time of writing this letter American poet Whitman (1819– 1892) had just had his book of poems *Leaves of Grass* published.

⑤ Signature: The author's name, and the date and location of letter writing should all be written clearly.

生词
New words

珍异	zhēnyì	wonderful
视而不见	shì ér bú jiàn	look without seeing
睿智	ruìzhì	wit and wisdom
横溢	héngyì	full
拜读	bàidú	read
喜不自胜	xǐ bú zì shèng	be delighted beyond measure
贫瘠	pínjí	sterile
吝啬	lìnsè	stingy
矫揉造作	jiǎo róu zào zuò	preciosity
疏懒	shūlǎn	lazy
平庸	píngyōng	mean
无与伦比	wú yǔ lún bǐ	incomparably
心花怒放	xīn huā nù fàng	be highly delighted
远见卓识	yuǎn jiàn zhuó shí	foresight and sagacity
激发	jīfā	inspire
鹏程万里	péng chéng wàn lǐ	have a long foreground
置疑	zhìyí	doubt
良师益友	liáng shī yì yǒu	benefactor
拜访	bàifǎng	visit

结构模板
The template of structure

贺信①

尊敬的□□：②

　　□□□。③

　　　　　　　　　　　　　　　　　　　　　□□□

　　　　　　　　　　　　　　　　　□□□□年□□月□□日 ④

模板格式说明

The template format explanation

① 标题:位置要居中。

Caption: This should be centred on the page.

② 称谓:标题下第一行顶格写。

Appellation: Written on the line below the caption without indenting.

③ 正文:段首空两格。行文中注意分清层次段落。

Text: The first line should indent two spaces. Paragraphs should be arranged clearly.

④ 署名:在信的右下方,发贺信人姓名在上,日期在下。

Signature: This should be written at the bottom right hand side of the page, beneath the text. The date should be written below the author's name.

练习 Exercises

1 顺藤摘瓜 Following the clues

按照例文和结构模板的提示,根据下面提供的材料,写一封贺信。

According to the example and the templet of structure, write a letter of congratulation based on the following material.

材料:

　　2005年10月12日,中国"神舟六号"载人宇宙飞船成功发射后,世界各地华侨华人纷纷发来贺电、贺信表示祝贺。请你以澳大利亚悉尼"中国和平统一促进会"的名义,向"神舟六号"全体工作人员写一封贺信。

2 照猫画虎
Follow the model

按照例文的"写法注释"和结构模板的"格式说明",试着给自己的同学或朋友写一份贺信。According to the writing notes in the example and the templet structure explanation, try to write a letter of congratulation to your classmate or friend.

第九课 履 历
Resume

Basic principles and aims
要点提示

1. 掌握履历的格式和语言特点。
   Master the format and language characteristics of resumes.
2. 基本掌握履历的写法。
   Master the basics of resume writing.

例文指路
Example guide

例文一

Example I

个人履历①

刘健,男。1968年7月14日生于江西省南昌市红光街10号,现在42岁,汉族人,已婚,一子四岁;妻在××大学音乐系任教。现住址:郑州市管城区世纪新村8单元302室。邮政编码:450292,电话号码:(0371)7745256。

主要经历:1987年毕业于××第一高级中学,同年考入××大学法律系,1991年

写法注释
Writing notes

① 用途:个人履历是用来真实记录自己成长、学习、工作经历的一种应用文。

第九课 履历

大学毕业后留校任教；1992年考入××大学研究生院法学系，1995年毕业，获法学硕士学位，同年被学校选派至美国××大学进修，1997年获法学博士学位，回国后到××大学任教至今。②

刘健
2010年3月4日 ③

Resume

Liu Jian, male. Born on July 14th, 1968 at No. 10 Hongguang St, Nanchang, Jiangxi Province, now 42 years old. Ethnic Han, married, with a four-year-old son; wife teaches in the Music Department of XX University. Present address is Room 302, unit 8, Shiji Xincun, Guancheng District, Zhengzhou. Zip code: 450292, telephone number: (0371) 7745256.

Educational history and employment experience: Graduated from XX No. 1 Senior Middle School in 1987, entered the Law Department of XX University the same year. Worked as a teacher after graduation in 1991;

② **正文**：要求实事求是地真实记录自己以往的经历。本例文正文分两部分，第一部分简要介绍了出生、家庭、住址等个人基本情况，第二部分依时间顺序记录了他的学习经历。履历语言要求简洁明了，真实准确。

③ **署名**：写明个人的姓名和写作履历的时间。

① Purpose: A resume is a written record of one's educational and employment history.

② Text: This should accurately reflect the writer's history. The example is divided into two parts, the first part briefly covers personal information such as date of birth, family, address, and other personal details. The second part is a chronological record of his educational history. The language is clear and precise.

③ Signature: The name and date should both be written.

entered the Law Department Graduate College of XX University in 1992, received a master's degree of law in 1995, and was then sent to XX University in America to take advanced courses in the same year; received a doctorate in law in 1997; has taught at XX University in China since then.

Liu Jian

March 4th, 2010

例文二
Example II

履历表①

何年何月至何年何月②	在何地何部门任何职	工作属性	证明人③
1980.9—1985.7	河南省荥阳市广武乡丁楼村	读书	丁贯中
1985.9—1988.7	荥阳市第一初级中学	读书	马玉珍
1988.9—1991.7	荥阳市第一高级中学	读书	楚 坤
1991.9—1995.7	郑州大学中文系	读书	郑 杰
1995.10—1997.8	荥阳市第四高级中学	教书	王 芳
1997.9 至今	郑州大学文化与传播学院	教书	张红生

Date	Place	Status	Reference
1980.9—1985.7	Dingloucun Guangwuxiang Xingyang, Henan Province	Student	Ding Guanzhong
1985.9—1988.7	Xingyang No. 1 Junior Middle School	Student	Ma Yuzhen
1988.9—1991.7	Xingyang No. 1 Senior Middle School	Student	Chu Kun
1991.9—1995.7	Chinese Department Zhengzhou University	Student	Zheng Jie
1995.10—1997.8	Xingyang No. 4 Senior Middle School	Teacher	Wang Fang
1997.9 至今	Culture and Communication College, Zhengzhou University	Teacher	Zhang Hongsheng

写法注释
Writing notes

① 这是一份表格式履历的写法。
② 时间上要求不能有空当。
③ 各项的填写都要求简洁、真实、准确。

① This is the layout of a resume form.
② It is required that there are no serious interregnums in the dates.
③ Each section must be completed clearly and accurately.

第九课 履历

生词 New words

履历	lǚlì	resume
任教	rènjiào	teach
留校	liúxiào	be appointed to work in a school one just graduated from
硕士	shuòshì	master
进修	jìnxiū	attend in advanced study
博士	bóshì	doctor

结构模板 The template of structure

履 历①

　　□□□。□□□□□□□□□□□□□□□□□□□□□□□□□□□□□□□□□□□□□□□。②

　　　　　　　　　　　　　　　　　　　　　　　□□□

　　　　　　　　　　　　　　　　　□□□□年□□月□□日③

模板格式说明

The template format explanation

① 标题：位置要居中。

Caption: This should be centred on the page.

② 正文：段首空两格。行文中注意分清层次段落。

Text: The first line should indent two spaces. Paragraphs should be arranged clearly.

③ 署名：在履历正文的右下方，署上姓名和成文时间。

Signature: This should be written at the bottom right hand side of the page, beneath the resume. The date should be written below the author's name.

练习 Exercises

1. 顺藤摘瓜
Follow the clues

按照例文一和结构模板的提示,根据自己的经历,写一份履历。

According to the example and the templet of structure, write a resume based on your own experience.

2. 照猫画虎
Follow the model

按照例文二设计表格,将自己的学习或工作经历制成一份表格式履历表。

According to the form in example two, write a resume form according to your study or working experience.

第十课 海 报
Poster

Basic principles and aims
要点提示

1. 掌握海报的格式。
   Master the format of posters.
2. 基本掌握海报的写法。
   Master the basics of poster writing.

例文指路 Example guide

例文一
Example I

海报①

为了提高广大同学的文艺鉴赏水平，特邀请南海大学著名教授赵志明来我校做"文艺鉴赏纵横谈"讲座，欢迎大家踊跃参加。②

时间：5月9日下午2点

地点：本校学术报告厅③

××大学学生会

2009年5月7日④

写法注释
Writing notes

① **用途**：海报是向公众报知、介绍文体赛事、学术报告、沙龙聚会等消息时使用的一种应用文体。

② **正文**：要求简要介绍活动的目的、名称、内容等。语言要求简洁明了，真实准确。

③ **时间、地点**：写明活动举行的具体时间和地点。要尽可能写具体、准确。

④ **署名**：写明活动的组织者名称和海报成文时间。

59

Poster

  In order to improve the students' appreciation and knowledge of literature and art, Zhao Zhiming of Nanhai University has been especially invited to come and give a lecture, "Free Talk on Appreciating Literature and art", all are welcome to come and participate.

Time: 2 p.m., May 9th

Place: School Auditorium

XX University Student Association

May 7th, 2009

① Purpose: A poster is used to inform people of events, such as sporting activities, literary and academic report, party etc.
② Text: This should briefly introduce the name, goal and outline of the activity. The language should be clear and concise.
③ Time and place: This should detail the time and place accurately.
④ Signature: The name of the activity organiser and the date of the poster's creation should be included.

例文二
Example II

中国潮大型文艺晚会海报①

晚会汇集国内外创作精英,特邀台湾歌坛明星潘安邦、东南亚十大歌星之一顾其华、民族唱法第一硕士彭丽媛、上海——巴黎通俗歌曲大赛国内金奖获得者杭天琪、广州黑马歌星幽默歌手赵世林等海内外著名歌星、舞星。

晚会融歌、舞、诗于一炉,气势宏大、规模空前、形式别具一格。②

演出时间、地点:5月15日、16日、17日晚7时30分于××体育馆(首场已满)。

售票时间、地点:4月10日起在五台山体育中心、和平电影院、延安剧场、人民剧场、解放电影院售个人票。③

联系人:李××

联系电话:55984238④

写法注释
Writing notes

① 标题:这份海报的标题写明了活动的具体名称,再加"海报"两字。

② 正文:要求简要介绍活动的目的、活动的名称、内容等。语言要求简洁明了,真实准确。

③ 时间、地点:写明活动举行的具体时间和地点。要尽可能写具体、准确。

④ 其他事项:写明活动的组织者及联系方式。

① Caption: The caption of this poster specifies the name of this activity and adds the two characters 海报 to the end of the name.

② Text: This should briefly introduce the name, goal and outline of the activity. The language should be clear and concise.

③ Time and place: Write the time and place that the activity will be held at. Be as accurate and detailed as possible.

④ Other items: Include the contact details of the event organiser.

The Chinese Tide Evening Performance

This event aims to gather together outstanding domestic and foreign creators, and especially welcomes Taiwanese singing sensation Pan Anbang, famed Southeast Asian top ten singer Gu Qihua, Peng Liyuan, the first Master of national song, the domestic winner of the gold medal in the Shanghai-Paris pop song tournament Hang Tianqi, Guangzhou black horse humorous singing king Zhao Shilin and many other famous singers and dancers from home and abroad. The party will blend song, dance and poetry with great momentum, on an unprecedented scale, in a unique and distinctive style.

Performance time and place: May 15th, 16th and 17th at 7.30 p.m. in xx Stadium. (The premiere show is already full).

Booking time and place: Tickets can be purchased from April 10th onwards at the Wutaishan Sports Center, Heping Movie Theater, Yan'an Theater, People's Theater and the Liberation Movie Theater.

Contact: Li × ×

Telephone: 55984238

生 词
New words

文艺	wényì	literary and art
鉴赏	jiànshǎng	appreciate
讲座	jiǎngzuò	lecture
踊跃参加	yǒngyuè cānjiā	participate actively
精英	jīngyīng	outstanding person
别具一格	bié jù yì gé	a distinctive style

第十课 海报

结构模板
The template of structure

海报①

　　□□。②

　　时间：□□□□□□
　　地点：□□□□□□③

□□□□□
□□□□年□□月□□日④

模板格式说明
The template format explanation

① 标题:位置要居中。

Caption: This should be centred on the page.

② 正文:段首空两格。行文中注意分清层次段落。

Text: The first line should indent two spaces. Paragraphs should be arranged clearly.

③ 时间、地点:在正文主体之下,前面空两格。

Time and place: This should be written under the text and preceded by two spaces.

④ 署名:如需写明活动组织者名称,在海报的右下方,署上组织者的名称和成文时间。

Signature: The name of the activity organiser and the date of the poster's creation should be written in the lower right hand side of the poster, underneath the text.

练习 Exercises

1. 画龙点睛
Complete the exercise

按照例文一和结构模板的提示,把下面的海报补充完整。

According to example one and the templet of structure, complete the following poster.

海报

为了_____,特举办_____

活动。请_____参加。

时间:_____

地点:_____

_____

_____年_____月_____日

2. 照猫画虎
Follow the model

按照例文二和结构模板的提示,请设计一则文艺活动海报。

According to example two and the templet of structure, design a literary activity poster.

第十一课　欢迎词
Welcome Speech

Basic principles and aims
要点提示

1. 了解欢迎词的用途。
   Understand the purpose of welcome speeches.
2. 熟悉欢迎词的结构和语言特点。
   Become familiar with the structure and the language characteristics of welcome speeches.
3. 基本掌握欢迎词的写法。
   Master the basics of writing welcome speeches.

例文指路
Example guide

例文
Example

欢迎词 ①

尊敬的各位来宾：②

　　今晚，我们有机会与史密斯教授欢聚一堂，十分荣幸。

　　史密斯先生是我们大家所熟悉的国际政治问题专家，他在研究国际政治问题方面取得了巨大成就，久负盛名。首先让

写法注释
Writing notes

① 用途：适用于在各种比较正式的社交场合，主人为接待或招待客人所作的表示欢迎的、热情友好的讲话。

② 称谓：也可以写成"尊敬的各位先生、女士"、"各位老师、同学们"等。

65

我代表今天出席会议的全体代表，对远道而来的贵宾表示热烈欢迎和敬意。

史密斯先生多年来一直关注世界形势的发展，他曾不止一次地访问非洲，对非洲的历史和现状了如指掌。今晚我们特别邀请他来与我们分享他对非洲局势的深入探讨和研究心得。

现在，让我们以热烈的掌声欢迎史密斯先生！③

Welcome Speech

Honoured guests,

It is with great honour tonight that we have the joyous opportunity of gathering with Professor Smith.

Professor Smith is a well-known expert on international politics, and has made great achievements in his long and distinguished career in researching international political issues. First, let me extend a warm welcome to him on behalf of all the representatives at today's

③ 正文：先对来宾表示欢迎之意；接着对来宾的身份、职位等情况进行简要介绍；然后对来宾的学术成就或工作成就等方面给予适当的正面评价；最后再一次以热情洋溢的方式对来宾表示欢迎，表达良好祝愿、希望等。

欢迎词语言要求要表达出对来宾的热情欢迎之意，用语要精当准确、恰到好处，言简意赅，篇幅短小。

① Purpose: A welcome speech is suitable for use on various official occasions, and expresses the host's welcome and appreciation for their guest.

② Appellation: 尊敬的各位先生女士，各位老师，同学们 etc. are usually used.

③ Text: This should begin with a welcome to the guest, which is then followed with a brief introduction to the guest, discussing their relevant history and achievements. Next, suitable remarks and praise should be made regarding the guest's achievements in their field. The speech should be ended by once again expressing a warm welcome to the guest, and wishing them all the best for the future.

The language of the welcome speech should be cordial and warm, and the wording appropriate to the occasion. It should not be overly effusive, but instead be more concise.

conference, and thank him for travelling so far to join us here.

Mr. Smith has closely followed developments in world events for many years now. He has visited Africa many times, and knows its history and current issues like the palm of his hand. Tonight, we invite him to share his thoughts, analysis and the conclusions he has come to over his years of research in the region.

Now, let's welcome Mr. Smith with a warm round of applause!

生 词
New words

欢聚一堂	huān jù yì táng	joyful gathering
久负盛名	jiǔ fù shèng míng	with a long esteemed reputation
热烈欢迎	rèliè huānyíng	warm welcome
了如指掌	liǎo rú zhǐ zhǎng	know sth like the palm of one's hand
局势	júshì	situation
心得	xīndé	attainment

结构模板
The template of structure

欢迎词①

尊敬的□□□:②

　　□□□□□□□□□。

　　□□□□□□□□□□□□□□□□□□□□□□□□□□□□□□□□。

　　□□□□□□□□□□□□□□□□□□□□□□□□□□□□□□□□□□□□□。③

模板格式说明

The template format explanation

① 标题:位置要居中。

　　Caption: This should be centred on the page.

② 称谓:在标题下第一行,顶格位置书写。

　　Appellation: Written on the line below the caption without indenting.

③ 正文:段首空两格。行文中注意分清层次段落。

　　Text: The first line should indent two spaces. Paragraphs should be arranged clearly.

Exercises

1 例文评析
Example analysis

利用你所学的欢迎词的有关写作知识,请对下面一则欢迎词的写法、格式、内容、语言等方面进行评析。

According to the welcome speech which you have learnt, analyze the writing, format, content, language and so on of the following welcome speech.

欢迎词

各位员工:

　　首先请我们用热烈的掌声欢迎远道而来的张正清律师。

　　张正清律师大家都不陌生,在5月与A公司侵权官司案中,张正清先生即是我方的辩护律师,他为打赢这场官司付出了很多的心血,我们向他表示诚挚的敬意和感谢。

　　为了促进我公司管理的制度化进程,也为了提高员工的法律意识,解决公司日常工作中的法律咨询问题,我们特从北京聘请了张先生做我们公司的法律顾问。我们相信以他的能力一定会达到一个满意的效果。今晚为了迎接他的到来,我们特备薄宴,为他洗尘。

　　再次欢迎张先生加盟我公司!

2 照猫画虎
Follow the model

按照例文和结构模板的提示，请写一份欢迎词。

According to the example and the templet of structure, write a welcome speech.

第十二课

一般书信
Ordinary Letter

Basic principles and aims
要点提示

1. 了解一般书信的写作格式特点。
   Understand the writing format characteristics of ordinary letters.
2. 熟悉一般书信的结构和语言特点。
   Become familiar with the structure and the language characteristics of ordinary letters.
3. 基本掌握一般书信的写法。
   Master the basics of ordinary letter writing.

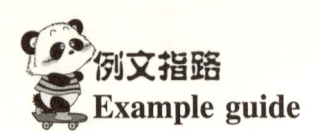

例文指路
Example guide

例文
Example

亲爱的爸爸、妈妈：①

你们还好吧！②

自从离开你们，不知不觉已经有半年了。每当工作结束，休息的时候，我脑海里总是浮现你们劳累的身影，感到十分愧疚。但是我一想到学习、工作的重要，不得不硬着心肠，放弃了侍奉你们的责任。我

写法注释
Writing notes

① **称谓**：根据收信人与自己的关系来确定称呼。如"敬爱的老师"、"尊敬的伯父"、"亲爱的安安"等等。

② **问候语**：可以写"您好！"、"你们好吧！"、"近来可好？"、"身体还好吧！"等等问候身体、近况、工

知道你们一定会原谅我的。

　　从我进厂至今,转眼已经有五个多月了。起初在货仓做些清洁和整理工作,后来我们组长看我做事勤快耐劳,又把我调到材料收发保管部。每日帮助收发各种材料,记载简单账务,种类复杂,计算单位很多,规格不一致,工作比以前繁忙,可是我学到不少新知识。管理员诚恳和气,待我很好,我自己也很奋力上进。

　　厂里工作紧张,时常加班,我处处谨慎,一点儿也不敢偷懒。厂里各种规矩,现在我都已经明白了,饮食起居自己也晓得保重,请你们不要挂念,肃此奉禀。③

　　敬叩
福安④

儿聪聪敬上
2009年5月12日⑤

第十二课　一般书信

作等情况的问候语,不拘一格,有多种写法。

③ **正文**：一般书信是为了交流思想、互通信息、沟通情况、磋商事宜所采用的一种书面谈话形式。此类信要求感情真挚、内容真实、语言真切、层次分明。

④ **致敬语**：有多种写法,可以根据与收信人的关系写不同的致敬语。如写给长辈、师长,多用"恭祝,金安"、"敬叩,安康"、"顺祝,教安"等等。也可以写上祝愿的话,如"祝你幸福安康！"、"期待你的回信！"、"永远想念你！"等等。

⑤ **署名**：写信人的姓名和写信时间。在姓名的前面一般加上与收信人的关系称呼或其他修饰语,如："女儿"、"侄"、"妻"、"你的爱人"、"永远爱你的"、"想念你的"等等。署名后面也可以加上适当的修饰语,如"敬上"、"草上"、"于上海"、"手书"等等。

① Appellation: The appellation is determined according to the relationship between the writer and receiver of the letter.

② Greeting: This can be 您好, 你们好吧, 近来可好 or 身体还好吧 etc. depending on the situation. Greetings are not limited to a specific type; many different types can be used.

③ Text: The ordinary letter reflects a conversational style, and is used to exchange ideas, share information, describe situations, and consult and advise on matters. This type of letter should be clearly written, containing solid and organised content.

Dear Father and Mother,

How are you?

Since I left you, half a year has flown by without my noticing. Whenever I finish work, and have a moment's repose, your tired faces always appear in my mind, and I feel ashamed. However, I have had to harden my heart to such images, and put aside my responsibility to serve you for now, as I concentrate on the important tasks of studying and working, and I know that you will forgive me for this.

More than five months have flown by since I entered the factory. At first I was working cleaning and tidying in the goods warehouse, then our group leader transferred me to the goods receiving and dispatching storage department because he thought I worked diligently and perseveringly. Everyday I help to receive and dispatch various goods and keep simple account records. There are many complexities such as different types of measurements, and unspecified quantities of goods; my job now is busier than it was before, but I'm gaining a lot of new knowledge. My manager is very genuine and friendly, and treats me very well, and I'm feeling very positive about everything.

Working in the factory is intense, and we often work overtime; I am trying to work hard and never be lazy. I have learned every rule in the factory and am able to take good care of myself here, so please don't be concerned about me.

Best Wishes!

Respectfully, your son Congcong

May 12th, 2009

④ Final salutation: The salutation depends on the relationship between the writer and receiver of the letter. When writing to elders or teachers for example, 恭祝金安, 敬叩安康 and 顺祝教安 etc. would be used, along with words indicating the writers good wishes for the receiver.

⑤ Signature: This should include the writer's name and date when the letter is written. A modifier may be added to indicate the relationship between the writer and the addressee, such as 女儿, 侄, 妻, 你的爱人, 永远爱你的 and 想念你的 etc. Other suitable modifiers following them are 敬上, 草上, 于上海 and 手书 etc.

第十二课 一般书信

生词
New words

脑海	nǎohǎi	mind
浮现	fúxiàn	appear
劳累	láolèi	tired
侍奉	shìfèng	serve
勤快	qínkuài	diligent
偷懒	tōulǎn	lazy
晓得	xiǎodé	know
挂念	guàniàn	concern

结构模板
The template of structure

□□□□□：①
　□□□□□□□□□！②
　　□□□
□□。
　　□□□
□□□□。③
　　□□
□□④
　　　　　　　　　　　　　　　　　　　　　　　□□　□□□
　　　　　　　　　　　　　　　　　　　　　　□□□□年□□月□□日⑤

模板格式说明

The templet format explanation

① 称谓：位于第一行顶格，后面用冒号。

Appellation: Written on the line below the caption without indenting, followed by a colon.

② 问候语:在称呼下第一行,前空两格。

Greeting: Written on the line below the appellation, preceded by two spaces.

③ 正文:段首空两格。行文中注意分清层次段落。

Text: The first line should be preceded by two spaces. Paragraphs should be arranged clearly.

④ 致敬语:在正文之下,第一行空两格,第二行顶格。如果是一句话的祝愿性的致敬语,在正文下空两格写,句末用感叹号。

Final salutation: This should be written below the text. The first line should be preceded by two spaces, and the second line should be preceded without any space. If it is a one-sentence phrase expressing good wishes, it should be written below the text and preceded by two spaces ended with an exclamation point.

⑤ 署名:在致敬语之下的右下方,姓名在上,日期在下。

Signature: This should be written at the bottom right hand side of the page, beneath the final salutation. The date should be written below the author's name.

练习 Exercises

1 例文评析
Example analysis

根据本课所掌握的一般书信的写作知识,对下面一封信的格式、写法、语言特点等进行评析。

According to the ordinary letter which you have learned, analyze the format, writing, and language characteristics of the following letter.

亲爱的妹妹:

　　几个月没有见面,你近来好吗?十分想念。

　　听说你这学期功课很少进步,今天我特地写信勉励你,希望你能诚心接受。

　　一个人若想将来成就事业,从小读书的时候,就要好好奠定基础,到了社会上才能

成器。趁你还在小学阶段,一定要下决心把各门功课学好,以便顺利进入初中、高中、大学,成为一个饱学之士,一个有用的人才。千万不要偷懒贪玩,遇到困难的问题,应该详求解答,不可马虎了事,如果不求上进因循下去,终究没有成功的一天。

　　古人说:"少壮不努力,老大徒伤悲。"望你能反省一下。及时努力学习,再不要浪费宝贵光阴,这点请你务必牢记。就聊到这,下次再谈。

　　祝你
进步

　　　　　　　　　　　　　　　　　　　　　　　兄　尚文　手书
　　　　　　　　　　　　　　　　　　　　　　　　　4月28日

2 照猫画虎
Follow the model

按照例文和结构模板的提示,给自己的家人或朋友写一封信。

According to the example and the templet of structure, write a letter to your family or a friend.

第十三课

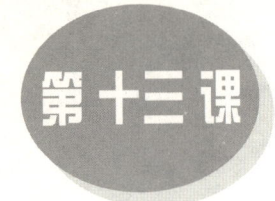

倡议书
Proposal

要点提示
Basic principles and aims

1. 了解倡议书的用途。
   Understand the purpose of proposals.
2. 熟悉倡议书的结构和语言特点。
   Be familiar with the structure and the language characteristics of proposals.
3. 基本掌握倡议书的写法。
   Master the basics of proposal writing.

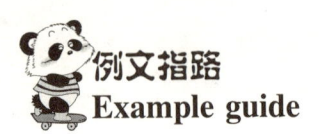

例文指路
Example guide

例文
Example

世界环境日《绿色宣言》倡议书①

所有爱好绿色、珍惜生命、关注人类未来命运的人们：②

今天，此时此刻，我们将以虔诚的声音诵读一个词汇：绿色。她是我们永远不变的希望，是我们世代延续的生机！

写法注释
Writing notes

① 用途及标题：倡议书是由个人或集体发起和倡导某种建议，用以共同完成某项任务或开展某种公益活动时而使用的一种应用文。

标题可以只写"倡议书"三个字，也可以像例文一样，由倡议内容和文种名称"倡议书"共同组成。

我们诵读,并将认真对待这个词汇所代表着的每一个事物:她是曾经孕育地球生命的海洋;她是曾经保护这生命得以成长的森林;她是曾经被这生命用最初的脚步行走的大地和用最初的智慧创造的艺术。她象征着我们最本质的财富。

她会让养育着数亿生命的耕地不会因为雨水和干旱而流失荒芜;她会保护蕴藏着现代文明的城市不再遭受野蛮风沙的侵袭;她会尽可能地保证我们健康的肌体渐渐远离病痛和伤害;她会让孩子们打开家门就能看到梦中的花园和草地。

在这个美丽的词汇之外,我们当然也懂得另外一些词汇的含义。我们知道,我们见到:厄尔尼诺、酸雨、污水、沙漠化……在一次次侵犯和报复中,提醒着我们所有的人。

因此,所有珍惜生命的人,所有关注人类未来命运的人,所有对我们生存的世界怀着热忱的人,为了我们共同的原则和理想,请和我们一起郑重地发出呼吁。

我们呼吁:珍惜每一滴水,每一棵树,每一块草坪,每一片土地,这将成为我们的常识,成为我们最朴素的品质。

让我们彼此提醒,让我们时刻都记得,一缕油烟,一粒沙尘,一节废电池,在不知不觉间就能改变世界,伤害我们自己。

让我们彼此教育,学会善待那些与人

② **称谓**:可以依照倡议的对象而确定适当的称呼,如"广大青少年朋友们:""广大的妇女同胞们:"等。有的倡议书也可不用称呼,而在正文中指出。

③ **正文**:倡议书正文的内容一般包括两个部分。

第一部分先写明发起倡议的背景、原因和目的。只有交待清楚倡议活动的原因以及当时的各种背景事实,并申明发布倡议的目的,人们才会理解和信服,才会自觉地行动。

第二部分写明倡议的具体内容和要求。这部分是倡议书的重点部分。倡议的内容一定要具体化,都需要响应者做什么事情,具体又有哪些要求,它的价值和意义都有哪些等,这些内容均需写明。

④ **结尾**:这部分要充分表现倡议者的决心和希望,也可以写出倡议者提出的建议。

⑤ **署名**:包括两项内容,先写明发出倡议的单位或个人名称,再注明发出倡议的时间。

① Purpose and caption: A proposal can be written by an individual or a collective to offer advice for project completions, and propose schemes for public and private benefit etc. The caption can either just include the three characters 倡议书 or the proposal name plus the three characters as is seen in the example.

② Appellation: This can be used to emphasize the heading of the proposal, for example 广大青少年朋友们, 广大的妇女同胞们

类共同享有自然的生灵,学会善待孩子们的想象,让他们有更多的机会懂得爱和珍惜。

让我们鼓励、尊重那些在风沙线上拼死斗争的人们,帮助那些为了让我们的生活充满绿色而付出代价的人们,支持那些将创造绿色当做事业的人们。

今天,此时此刻,我们将以虔诚的声音诵读这个词汇。这声音将被你们倾听;这声音将被你们重复;这声音将被你们化作行动。③

我们相信,有一天,绿色会铺满中国辽阔的大地!④

参加倡议的媒体:人民日报、读者、京华时报、家庭、女友、北京晚报、文摘报、中国大学生等100家报刊杂志

6月5日⑤

etc. Some proposals do not need this, instead the target readers will be mentioned in the text.

③ Text: This usually consists of two parts. The first part describes the background, reason and purpose of the proposal. These need to be explained well, with the background facts laid out clearly and the purpose described in detail, so that people will fully understand and be willing to adopt the proposal. The second part outlines the content and requirements of the proposal. The content must be solid and the requirements clearly defined, so that it can be seen what each requirement is needed for, and what value they will add to the overall result.

④ Ending: This should express the wishes and determination or suggestions of the proposal writer.

⑤ Signature: This should include the name of the individual or group making the proposal, and the date of its creation.

"Green Declaration" Proposal on International Environment Day

To all people who value the environment, treasure life, and are concerned about the future of human life:

Today, at this very moment, we devoutly read aloud this one word: green. She is our unchanging eternal hope, the spirit we give to continuing generations.

We read and treat everything the word represents with the utmost care: she is the sea from which life on earth begins; she is the forest which protects life's growth; she is the earth on which life's primal step is walked, and its primal arts created. She symbolises our most intrinsic treasure.

She will prevent the tillable fields from being destroyed by damaging rain and drought; she will protect the modern cities from wild sandstorms; she will do her best to keep our bodies from feeling pain and harm; she will let children open their doors to see the gardens and grasslands they have seen in their nightly dreams.

Besides this beautiful word, there are other words whose meaning we also understand. We both know and have seen: El Nino, acid rain, sewage, desertification...such words remind us all of the infringements and retaliation occurring again and again against our earth.

So to all people who treasure life, who are concerned with the future of humanity, who have a passion for our world, we today earnestly call on you to unite with us in our common principles and ideals.

We call on all to cherish every drop of water, every tree, every patch of grass, and every field, and make it our common sense and plainest quality.

Let us remind each other that at any moment a wisp of smoke, a particle of dust, a wasted battery all have the power to unthinkingly change our world and cause us harm.

Let us educate each other, so that we can learn to treat all creatures that share nature with humans equally, let us learn to treat the imagination of children with more kindness and openness and give them more chances to understand how to love and treasure our planet.

Let us encourage and respect those who struggle on the edge of the desert, help those who strive to make our lives full of green, and support those who consider making the world a greener place their calling.

Today, at this very moment, we devoutly read aloud this one word. It will be heard by you, repeated by you, and then turned into action by you.

We believe that one day green will cover the extensive lands of China!

This proposal was a joint initiative of: Renmin Daily, Readers, Jinghua Times, Family, Woman Friend, Beijing Evening News, Digest Paper, Chinese College Students and over a hundred other newspapers, periodicals and magazines.

生词
New words

倡议	chàngyì	propose
虔诚	qiánchéng	devout
延续	yánxù	continue
荒芜	huāngwú	desolation
蕴藏	yùncáng	contain
野蛮	yěmán	wild
侵袭	qīnxí	attack
热忱	rèchén	zeal
郑重	zhèngzhòng	earnestly
呼吁	hūyù	call on
倾听	qīngtīng	listen
辽阔	liáokuò	extensive

第十三课 倡议书

结构模板
The template of structure

□□□□□倡议书①
□□□□□□:②
　　□□□。③
　　□□□□□□□。④

　　　　　　　　　　　　　　　　　　　　　　　□□□□□
　　　　　　　　　　　　　　　　　　　　□□□□年□□月□□日⑤

模板格式说明
The template format explanation

① 标题:位置要居中。

Caption: This should be centred on the page.

② 称谓:在标题下第一行,顶格写,后面加冒号。

Appellation: Written on the line below the caption without indenting, followed by a colon.

③ 正文:段首空两格。正确使用标点符号,行文中注意分清层次段落。

Text: The first line should indent two spaces. Paragraphs should be arranged clearly.

④ 结尾:发出的希望要求等,在正文下行,前面空两格。如果是提出的建议,可以分条列项写出。

Ending: This should be written on the line below the text, and be preceded by two spaces. If it includes advice and suggestions it may be written in point form.

⑤ 署名:在全文右下角位置,单位名称或个人姓名在上面一行,日期在下面一行。

81

Signature: This should be written at the bottom right hand side of the page. The date should be written below the signature.

练习 Exercises

1 例文评析 Example analysis

请利用你所学的倡议书的有关写作知识,对下面一则倡议书的写法、格式、内容、语言等方面进行评析。

According to the proposal which you have learnt, analyze the writing, format, content, language and so on of the following proposal.

把遗体交给医学界利用的倡议书

人的遗体的解剖和其他利用,对医学研究和医学教育的发展作用很大。可惜由于种种旧思想的影响,遗体捐赠在中国至今还很不流行,致使大量有用之物弃于无用之地,深为可惜。

现在医学界和其他方面的先进人士已为遗体利用做出榜样,但究竟还是杯水车薪,远远不能满足需要。我们在下面签名的共产党员,自愿学习他们这种真正为人民服务直到死后的高尚品格,特向全国志同道合之士提出倡议。

遗体可利用范围很广,包括病理解剖、制作标本、教学人体解剖、向病人移植所必需的尚健全的组织,等等。我们不向广大群众提出这种要求,即使对共产党员也不作任何勉强,悉听自愿。这与提倡火葬或在火葬前后举行某些被认为必要的仪式毫不矛盾。因为遗体利用后的部分仍须火化,火葬能节约大量耕地、木材,并避免其他各种浪费、陋俗的好处全都同样保存了。我们只得行使个人法定的自由,既不勉强任何别人,也不大肆宣传,相信不致造成误解和妨碍火葬的推广。就如我们的先行者这样做了,在报纸上发表了,并未造成这种影响一样。我们征集签名的范围有限,但签名者仍然很多,这里只发表了很小一部分,以免使人觉得我们要"制造"什么"声势"。对此,希望已签名而这里没有发表的同志和愿签名而未受我们征集的同志谅解。凡是签名的人,都决心在生前做好自己家属的工作。

杨尚昆	胡乔木	余秋里	谷牧	陈丕显	章蕴	周扬
胡立教	林涧青	钱学森	钱三强	韩宁夫	马海德	贺敬之
沈困洛	吴英	于光远	艾青	李锐	邓力群	胡绳
钱信忠	王忍之	陈国栋等				

2 照猫画虎
Follow the model

按照例文和结构模板的提示，请根据下面提供的材料写一份节约用水的倡议书。
According to the example and the templet of structure, write a proposal for saving water based on the following material.

为了缓解世界范围内的水资源供需矛盾，根据联合国《21世纪议程》第十八章有关水资源保护、开发、管理的原则，1993年1月18日，联合国第四十七次大会通过了193号决议，决定从1993年开始，确定每年的3月22日为"世界水日"。决议提请各国政府根据自己的国情，在这一天举办一些具体的宣传活动，以提高公众节水意识。

1996年，由水问题专家学者和相关国际机构组成的世界水理事会成立，并且决定在世界水日前后每隔3年举行一次大型国际会议，这就是世界水论坛会议。

历年世界水日的主题为：1994年，关心水资源是每一个人的责任；1995年，女性和水；1996年，解决城市用水之急；1997年，世界上的水够用吗？1998年，地下水——无形的资源；1999年，让每个人都生活在下游；2000年，21世纪的水；2001年，水与健康；2002年，水为发展服务；2003年，未来之水；2004年，水与灾害；2005年，生命之水；2006年，水与文化；2007年，水利发展与和谐社会；2008年，涉水卫生；2009年，跨界水——共享的水、共享的机遇。

前不久，联合国环境署已发出警告：人类在石油危机之后，下一个危机就是水。曾有人说过："如果人类继续破坏和浪费水资源，那么人类看到的最后一滴水将是自己的眼泪。"

第十四课　演讲稿
Speech Manuscript

Basic principles and aims
要点提示

1. 了解熟悉演讲稿的结构和语言特点。
   Understand and become familiar with the structure and the language characteristics of speech manuscripts.
2. 基本掌握演讲稿的写法。
   Master the basics of writing speech manuscripts.

例文指路
Example guide

例文
Example

我也是"义和团"
　　——马克·吐温在纽约的演讲①

尊敬的各位女士、先生们：②

　　我想，要我到这里来讲话，并不是因为把我看做一位教育专家。如果是那样，就会显得你们缺乏卓越的判断，并且仿佛是要提醒我别忘记我自己的弱点。

　　我坐在这里思忖着，终于想到了我之

写法注释
Writing notes

① 用途及标题：演讲稿就是指演讲者为表达自己的见解和主张，针对特定的时间、环境和听众，借助于有声语言和态势语言，以议论抒怀为主要表现形式而写作的演讲文稿。又称为讲演稿或演讲辞。

　　演讲稿的标题在写法上与一般文章的标题相同。可以是单行标题，也可以像本例文一样，所以被邀请到这里来,是有两个原因。一个原因是让我这个曾在大洋之上漂流的不幸的旅客懂得一点你们这个团体的性质与规模,让我懂得,世界上除了我以外,还有别的一些人正在做有益于社会的事,从而对我有所启迪。另一个原因是你们之所以邀请我,是为了通过对照来告诉我,教育如果得法,会有多大的成效。

尊敬的主席刚才说,曾在巴黎博览会上获得赞扬的有关学校的图片已经送往俄国,俄国政府对此深表感谢——这对我来说,倒是非常诧异的事。因为还只是一个钟点以前,我在报上读到一段新闻,一开头便说:"俄国准备实行节约。"我倒是没有料到会有这样的事。我当即想,要是俄国实行了节约,能把眼下派到中国东北去的三万军队召回国,让他们在和平生活中安居乐业,那对俄国来说是多大的好事。

我还想,这也是德国应该毫不拖延干的事,法国以及其他在中国派有军队的国家都应该跟着干。

为什么不让中国摆脱那些外国人,他们尽在她的土地上捣乱。如果他们都能回到老家去,中国这个国家将是中国人多么美好的家园啊!既然我们并不准许中国人到我们这儿来,我愿郑重声明:让中国人自己去决定,哪些人可以到他们那里去,那

写成双行标题,一般正标题是虚题,提示主题意义、高度概括内容,下面的副标题是实题,起补充说明的作用。标题拟定要与演讲内容紧密联系,标题要求新颖、生动、富有表现力,这样不仅能在演讲前造成悬念,而且能在演讲结束后给听众留下永久记忆。

② **称谓**:依据听众对象的类型成份拟定称谓,称谓要基本概括所有听众。如:"尊敬的主席先生,女士们、先生们",或"尊敬的老师,亲爱的同学们"等等。

③ **正文**:正文通常由开头、主体、结尾三部分构成。

开头开门见山,点明主题,亮出自己的观点,还要引人入胜,吸引听众的注意力。

主体部分要有一定的逻辑性,或以时间为序展开,或以因果、并列等逻辑关系安排内容顺序,内容较庞杂的还可以列出小标题。这部分是演讲稿写作的重点和难点。

结尾部分是演讲最精彩,最高潮的部分,是全文的收束部分,或与开头响应,或重申自己的主张、观点、看法,或发出呼吁,提出希望等等。

④ **署名**:包括两项内容,先写明演讲者的姓名,再注明演讲的时间。

① Purpose and caption: Speech manuscripts should express the writer's views and opinions with the help of vocal voices and body languages, and be aimed at specific audiences, environments, or address certain important

便是谢天谢地的事了。

外国人不需要中国人,中国人也不需要外国人。在这一点上,我任何时候都是和义和团站在一起的。义和团是爱国者,他们爱他们自己的国家胜过爱别的民族的国家。我祝愿他们成功。义和团主张要把我们赶出他们的国家。我也是义和团,因为我也主张把他们赶出我们的国家。

我继续读俄国电讯,我梦想的世界和平随之消失了。电讯上说,保持军队所需的巨额费用使得节约非实行不可。因而政府决定,为了维持这个军队,必须削减公立学校的经费。这是一个多荒谬的主意啊! 而我们则认为,国家的伟大来自公立学校。

试看历史怎样在全世界范围内重演,这是多么奇怪。我记得,当我还是密西西比河上一个小孩子的时候,曾有同样的事发生过。有一个镇子也曾主张停办公立学校,因为那太费钱了。有一位老农站起来说,他们不会省下什么钱,因为每关闭一所学校,就得多修造一座牢狱。

这如同把一条狗身上的尾巴用做饲料来喂养这条狗。它肥不了。我看,支持学校要比支持监狱强。

你们这个协会的活动,和沙皇及他的全体臣民比起来,显得具有更高的智慧。这

periods in time. The language should be expressive and moving. This type of writing is also called 讲演稿 or 演讲辞 etc.

The captions of speech manuscripts are written in the same style as those of common pieces of writing. They may be single or double line. In this example, the main caption is the nominal title and gives an overview of the topic at hand, while the subheading provides more information and background.

The title of the speech should be closely related to its content, and should employ language that will grab the attention of the audience, and engage their interest so that a suspense is provided before the speech and after it memory leaves.

② Appellation: This needs to be general enough to encompass the entire audience. Commonly used are 尊敬的主席先生,女士们,先生们 or 尊敬的老师,亲爱的同学们 etc.

③ Text: This generally includes an introduction, a main body, and a conclusion.

The introduction is straight-forward and introduces the main point of the speech. It should make the opinions of the speechwriter clear, and grab the audience's attention.

The body needs to develop in a logical manner. The content needs to be clearly laid out, if

倒不是过奖的话,而是说的我的心里话。③

马克·吐温

1901年×月×日④

I Am a Boxer

Mark Twain's Speech in New York

Dear ladies and gentlemen:

I don't suppose that I am called here as an expert on education, for that would show a lack of foresight on your part and a deliberate intention to remind me of my shortcomings.

As I sat here looking around for an idea it struck me that I was called for two reasons. One was to do good to me, a poor unfortunate traveler on the world's wide ocean, by giving me a knowledge of the nature and scope of your society and letting me know that others beside myself have been of some use in the world. The other reason that I can see is that you have called me to show by way of contrast what education can accomplish if administered in the right sort of doses.

Your worthy president said that the school pictures, which have received the admiration of the world at the Paris Exposition, have been sent to Russia, and this was a compliment from that Government—which is very surprising to me. Why, it is only an hour since I read a cablegram

necessary subheadings may be used. It should also coordinate with both the introduction and conclusion. This is the most important part of the speech, where the arguments and positions are articulated in detail.

The conclusion is the most remarkable part and the climax. It concludes the speech, and should refer back to the introduction, to reaffirm the views, opinions and arguments of the speech.

④ Signature: This should include the speaker's name and the date the speech was given.

in the newspapers beginning "Russia Proposes to Retrench." I was not expecting such a thunderbolt, and I thought what a happy thing it will be for Russians when the retrenchment will bring home the thirty thousand Russian troops now in Manchuria, to live in peaceful pursuits.

I thought this was what Germany should do also without delay, and that France and all the other nations in China should follow suit.

Why should not China be free from the foreigners, who are only making trouble on her soil? If they would only all go home, what a pleasant place China would be for the Chinese! We do not allow Chinamen to come here, and I say in all seriousness that it would be a graceful thing to let China decide who shall go there.

China never wanted foreigners any more than foreigners wanted Chinamen, and on this question I am with the Boxers every time. The Boxer is a patriot. He loves his country better than he does the countries of other people. I wish him success. The Boxer believes in driving us out of his country. I am a Boxer too, for I believe in driving him out of our country.

When I read the Russian despatch further my dream of world peace vanished. It said that the vast expense of maintaining the army had made it necessary to retrench, and so the Government had decided that to support the army it would be necessary to withdraw the appropriation from the public schools. This is a monstrous idea to us. We believe that out of the public school grows the greatness of a nation.

It is curious to reflect how history repeats itself the world over. Why, I remember the same thing was done when I was a boy on the Mississippi River. There was a proposition in a township there to discontinue public schools because they were too expensive. An old farmer spoke up and said if they stopped the schools they would not save anything, because every time a school was closed a jail had to be built.

It's like feeding a dog on his own tail. He'll never get fat. I believe it is better to support schools than jails.

第十四课 演讲稿

The work of your association is better and shows more wisdom than the Czar of Russia and all his people. This is not much of a compliment, but it's the best I've got in stock.

Mark Twain

Month Day, 1901

生词 New words

思忖	sīcǔn	ponder
漂流	piāoliú	drift
诧异	chàyì	surprising
安居乐业	ān jū lè yè	live in peaceful pursuits
拖延	tuōyán	delay
捣乱	dǎoluàn	make trouble
谢天谢地	xiè tiān xiè dì	grateful
削减	xuējiǎn	retrench
牢狱	láoyù	jail
饲料	sìliào	feed

结构模板 The template of structure

□□□□□□□ ①

□□□□□□: ②

　　□□□□□□□□□□□□□□□□□□□□□□□□□□□□□□□□□□□□□□□。

　　□□

□□□□□□□□□□□□□□□□□□。

　　□□□□□□□□□□□□□□□□□□□□□□□□□□□□□□□□□□□□□。③

□□□□□
□□□□年□□月□□日 ④

模板格式说明
The template format explanation

① 标题：位置要居中。

Caption: This should be centred on the page.

② 称谓：在标题下第一行，顶格写，后面加冒号。

Appellation: Written on the line below the caption without indenting, followed by a colon.

③ 正文：段首空两格。行文中注意分清层次段落。

Text: The first line should indent two spaces. Paragraphs should be arranged clearly.

④ 署名：在全文右下角位置，姓名在上面一行，日期在下面一行。

Signature: This should be written at the bottom right hand side of the page. The date should be written below the signature.

第十四课 演讲稿

1 例文评析
Example analysis

根据所学的演讲稿的写法和格式要求，评析下面的演讲稿在写法和语言上有什么优点。

According to the writing and format of the speech manuscript, analyse the advantages of the following speech's writing and language.

办公室主任竞聘演讲稿

各位领导、各位老师：

　　我首先感谢领导、同志们的信任和支持,给我这个机会参加竞职演讲。我叫赵世杰,现年41岁,大学本科学历,讲师职称。1996年8月担任××县成教中心办公室主任职务,1999年9月调到××县第三高级中学工作。我竞聘的岗位是办公室主任。我之所以竞聘这个职位,是因为我具有以下四个优势：

　　一是有较为扎实的专业知识。自参加工作以来,我始终不忘记读书,勤钻研,善思考,多研究,不断地丰富自己、提高自己,现在又参加了研究生课程班的学习。我先后承担过电大班、自考班、函授班、小教专科的《政治经济学》,中专班的政治、哲学、经济常识,干训班的教育理论等课的教学任务,2005年获全市中师教学"五项全能"比赛二等奖,2007年获全省中师政治优质课一等奖,先后有3篇教学教研论文在省市级杂志公开发表,参加过省《中师政治试题精选》一书的编写工作。

　　二是有较为丰富的实践经验。从1996年开始一直从事学校办公室工作,深知办公室在学校工作中的地位、作用,知道办公室的职责、任务和规范,明白办公室工作人员所必备的素质和要求,悟出了一些搞好办公室工作的方法策略,在宣传学校、参谋决策、日常服务、沟通协调、信息传递等方面做了一些力所能及的工作,取得了一定的成绩。如：干训、继教方面的经验材料在省市都产生过一定的影响,学校档案建设获省二级先进。

　　三是有较强的工作能力。我在日常生活和工作中注意不断地加强个人修养,以"明明白白做人,实实在在做事"为信条,踏实干事,诚实待人。经过多年学习和锻炼,自己的写作能力、组织协调能力、判断分析能力、领导部署能力都有了很大提高,能够胜任办公室工作。

　　四是有较好的年龄优势。我正值不惑之年,身体健康,精力旺盛,敬业精神强,能

够全身心地投入到自己所热爱的工作当中去。

假若我能够竞争上岗，我打算从以下几个方面改进办公室工作，提高办公室工作档次。

（一）科学规范地做好日常事务工作。学校办公室承担着文秘、人事、宣传报道、档案管理、文件、接待、车辆管理等工作，是信息传递、政策落实、上下内外沟通的窗口，是为学校教学工作起辅助作用的综合部门，既要承担琐碎的事务，又要参与政务。我将根据实际情况，进行合理分工，合理调度，认真落实岗位责任制，确保办公室事务性工作井然有序。

（二）搞好综合协调，确保学校政令畅通。及时传达贯彻学校决策，加强督办检查，促进学校各项决策的落实。认真、科学地搞好领导与领导、处室与处室之间的沟通协调工作，避免互相扯皮、推诿、出现工作空档，确保学校以教学为中心，各方面通力合作，默契配合，步调一致，共同完成建校大业。

（三）当好参谋助手，服务校长决策。及时准确地掌握学校各方面的工作动态，及时地向学校领导反馈各方面的信息，注重调查分析，主动为领导献计献策，对各种情况进行科学的分析和判断，为领导决策提供可靠的依据。对外广泛宣传学校，提高知名度，树立良好形象。

（四）加强个人修养，练好基本功。从事办公室工作光荣而辛苦，需要有强烈的事业心和责任感，需要有较强的工作能力和工作艺术。我将不断地加强学习，坚决服从组织安排，顾全大局，维护学校班子团结，维护领导形象，调动办公室全体工作人员的积极性，团结办公室人员一道共同搞好工作，提高服务质量，力争在服务中显示实力，在工作中形成动力，在创新中增加压力，在与人交往中凝聚合力。

领导、老师们，我有信心、有决心搞好学校办公室工作，愿与大家共创美好的未来，迎接××三中辉煌灿烂的明天。

谢谢大家！

赵世杰
2009年8月10日

2 照猫画虎
Follow the model

利用你所学的演讲稿的有关写作知识,参考练习一中的例文,请自拟题目写一篇竞争上岗的演讲稿。

According to the speech manuscript you have learnt, and referring to the example in exercise I, write a speech manuscript about competing for work.

第十五课

邀请函
Invitation Letter

Basic principles and aims
要点提示

1. 了解邀请函的用途。
   Understand the purpose of invitation letters.
2. 熟悉邀请函的结构和语言特点。
   Become familiar with the structure and language characteristics of invitation letters.
3. 基本掌握邀请函的写法。
   Master the basics of writing invitation lettes.

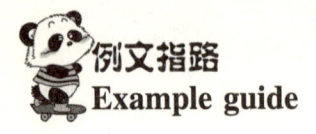

例文指路
Example guide

例文一
Example I

"网络时代的德育"研讨会邀请函①

李玉女士：②

　　网络时代的到来给学校德育工作带来了新的机遇和挑战。国家有关部门非常重视，社会各界十分关注，业内人士尤感忧虑。为此，中国教育报刊社继续教育中心将举办全国"网络时代的德育"研讨会。

写法注释
Writing notes

① **用途及标题**：邀请函是行政机关、企事业单位、社会团体或个人邀请有关人士参加某项活动或事宜时使用的一种专用书信。

　　标题可以只写"邀请函"三个字，也可以像例文一样，由活动内容和文种名称"邀请函"共同组成。

一、研讨会主要内容：1. 网络时代中小学德育面临的机遇和挑战。2. 网络时代中小学生的价值观。3. 如何把握网上育人的主动权。4. 网络时代教师、学生的心理特征。5. 网络德育模式的构建。6. 中小学生网络道德的培养。7. 网络时代的德育评价。8. 网站管理和网络内容的充实完善。9. 参观珠江三角洲地区学校及德育网站建设。

二、地点、时间：广东——珠海；6月3日—6月7日（6月2日全天报到）。

三、参加会议人员：各级教育行政部门领导、基础教育处及科研部门，各大、中、小学校长、书记，政教处及网站管理人员等。

四、相关事宜：

1. 会议拟邀请教育部有关部门领导、国内权威专家并作专题报告。免费发放相关资料。

2. 联系方式

电话报名：010—85983272

传真：010—85932393

信函报名：中国教育报刊社继续教育
　　　　　中心

地址：北京市海淀区展春园22号

邮编：100083 ③

欢迎参与！④

中国教育报刊社

② **称谓**：可以依照被邀请的对象而确定适当的称呼，如"尊敬的××先生（女士）："、"尊敬的××教授："、"××公司领导："等。

③ **正文**：邀请函的正文内容通常要写出举办活动的目的、活动内容、活动时间、活动地点、活动方式、邀请对象及联系办法等。活动的各种事宜务必在邀请函中写清楚、写周详。

④ **结尾**：结尾处要求写上礼节性的邀请语，如"恳请光临"、"致以敬意"等等。

⑤ **署名**：包括两项内容，先写明发出邀请的单位名称或个人姓名，再注明发出邀请的时间。

继续教育中心

××××年×月×日 ⑤

An invitation to the Discussion "Moral Education in the Internet Age"

Ms Li Yu,

  The coming of the internet age has brought new opportunities and challenges to moral education in schools. The related national department attaches great importance to this, all circles of society are paying earnest attention to this, and insiders are especially worried about this. Therefore the China Education Newspapers and Magazines Office Re-education Center has decided to hold a national forum on "Moral Education in the Internet Age".

  First, the topics covered in the forum will be thus: 1. The opportunities and challenges that face moral education in middle and primary schools in the internet age. 2. The values of middle and primary school students in the internet

① Purpose and caption: An invitation letter can be used by administrations, businesses, public organisations and individuals to invite people to attend activities and events. The caption should be related to the event, and include either the three characters 邀请函 only or the content plus the three characters, as is seen in the example.

② Appellation: This should be appropriate to the invitee, for example 尊敬的 xx 先生、女士, 尊敬的 xx 教授, xx 公司领导 etc.

③ Text: This section includes the aim of the activity or event, the time and location it will be held, an overview of its contents, and the name and contact details of the organiser. Everything should be written clearly and comprehensively.

④ Ending: A polite phrase such as 恳请光临 or 致以敬意 etc. should be used to end the invitation.

⑤ Signature: This should include the name of the inviting individual or organisation, and the date of the invitation's writing.

age. 3. How to fully maximise the opportunity to teach students via the internet. 4. The psychological characteristics of teachers and students in the internet age. 5. The construction of moral education plans on the internet. 6. The training of middle and primary school students on internet morals. 7. The judgement on moral education in the internet age. 8. Website management and the building and improvement of content on the internet. 9. Visiting schools and moral education websites construction in the Pearl River Delta area.

Secondly, the forum shall be held in Zhuhai, Guangdong; June 3rd — June 7th (registration will occur all day on June 2nd).

Thirdly, attending the forum will be various educational administrative department heads, the basic education department, the scientific research department, the principals, secretaries, political education department and website managers of colleges, middle schools and primary schools.

Fourthly, in regards to the practicalities of the forum:

1. The forum plans to invite the leaders of different education departments, and various experts to deliver talks on the fields of expertise. All related materials will be distributed freely.

2. Contact details.

To register by phone: 010 – 85983272

Fax: 010 – 85932393

To register by mail:

China Education Newspapers and Magazines Office Re-education Center

22 Zhanchunyuan St.

Haidian District

Beijing

100083

We welcome your participation!

    China Education Newspapers and Magazines Office Re-education Center

    Month / Day / Year

例文二
Example Ⅱ

邀请函①

××先生：②

  为了纪念王××先生诞辰一百周年，订于6月5日下午3时在学校学术报告厅举行"纪念王××先生诞辰一百周年学术研讨会"。素仰先生对王××学术研究成就卓著，誉满海内，我们恳切希望先生届时能光临指教，在大会上作学术报告。如承应允，希即赐复，以便安排，十分感激。③

  此致

敬礼④

××大学哲学系
2009年5月10日⑤

附：会议日程安排说明一份。⑥

写法注释
Writing notes

① **标题**：标题可以只写"邀请函"三个字，像这篇例文一样，也有些标题是由活动内容和文种名称"邀请函"共同组成。

② **称呼**：可以依照被邀请的对象而选用适当的称呼，如"尊敬的××先生（女士）："、"尊敬的××教授："、"××公司领导："等。

③ **正文**：邀请函的正文内容通常要写出举办活动的目的、活动内容、活动时间、活动地点、活动方式、邀请对象及联系办法等。活动的各种事宜务必在邀请函中写清楚、写周详。

④ **结尾**：结尾处可以写"此致，敬礼"等固定用语，也可以写上礼节性的邀请语，如"恳请光临"、"欢迎参加"等等。

⑤ **署名**：包括两项内容，先写明发出邀请的单位名称或个人姓名，再注明发出邀请的时间。

⑥ **附件**：有的邀请函在正文简单介绍活动时间、地点等内容，详细的活动相关事宜，会以附件的形式，同邀请函一同发出。附件一般是此项活动的详细的说明、通知、介绍等。

① Caption: The caption can include the content or only the three characters 邀请函, as is seen in the example.

② Appellation: This should be appropriate to the invitee, for example 尊敬的××先生/女士, 尊敬的××教授, ××公司领导 etc.

Invitation Letter

Mr xxx:

  To commemorate the one hundredth birthday of Mr. Wang XX, a conference on "Commemorating the one hundredth birthday of Mr. Wang XX" will be held in the Academic Hall at 3p.m. June 5th. We have long known of your high reputation, and heard of your great achievements in the field of research on Wang XX, and we sincerely hope that you will honour us with your presence and assent to give a speech at the conference. We hope that you will reply as soon as possible so that we may make the necessary arrangements. Thank you.

  Best Wishes!

Philosophy Department XX University
10th May 2009

Attached is a copy of the conference schedule.

③ Text: This section includes the aim of the activity or event, the time and location it will be held, an overview of its contents, and the name and contact details of the organiser. Everything should be written clearly and comprehensively.

④ Ending: A polite phrase such as 此致敬礼 or 恳请光临，欢迎参加 etc. should be used to end the invitation.

⑤ Signature: This should include the name of the inviting individual or organisation, and the date of the invitation's writing.

⑥ Attachment: Some invitations include more detailed information about the event, for example an itinerary of events, in an added attachment to the invitation.

实用汉语写作进阶(中级)

生词 New words

邀请	yāoqǐng	invite
机遇	jīyù	opportunity
挑战	tiǎozhàn	challenge
忧虑	yōulǜ	be worried
构建	gòujiàn	construction
诞辰	dànchén	birthday
素	sù	often
仰	yǎng	admire
卓著	zhuōzhù	outstanding
应允	yīngyǔn	assent

结构模板 The template of structure

邀请函①

□□□□□□□:②

　□□。③

　□□□□□□□□□。④

　　　　　　　　　　　□□□□
　　　　　　　□□□□年□□月□□日⑤

　□□□□□□□⑥

100

模板格式说明

The template format explanation

① 标题：位置要居中。

Caption: This should be centred on the page.

② 称谓：在标题下第一行，顶格写，后面加冒号。

Appellation: Written on the line below the caption without indenting, followed by a colon.

③ 正文：段首空两格。行文中注意分清层次段落。

Text: The first line should indent two spaces. Paragraphs should be arranged clearly.

④ 结尾：如果是"此致，敬礼"，写法是"此致"前空两格，"敬礼"在下一行顶格写。如果是其他礼节性邀请语，格式是在正文下一行，前空两格。

Ending: If the phrase 此致敬礼 is used to end the invitation, then 此致 is written beneath the text and preceded by two spaces, and 敬礼 is written on the line beneath that without indenting. If another phrase is used, then it is written on the line below the text and preceded by two spaces.

⑤ 署名：在全文右下角位置，姓名在上面一行，日期在下面一行。

Signature: This should be written at the bottom right hand side of the page. The date should be written below the signature.

⑥ 附件：位于署名下一行，先写上"附："，或写为"附件："，冒号后再写上附件的名称。

Attachment: This occurs on the line below the signature. It begins with 附： or 附件：, which is then followed by the name of the attachment.

练习 Exercises

1 照猫画虎 Follow the model

利用你所学的邀请函的有关写作知识,请将下面一则邀请函的内容补充完整。
According to the invitation letter which you have learnt, complete the following invitation letter.

_____

_____先生:

　　为了_____,我们学校决定于____年____月____日____时,在_____举行_____活动。久闻您_____,我们恳切邀请您能届时光临,并请您_____

_____

_____

　　附件:_____。

2 病例诊断 Example analysis

根据所学的邀请函的写法和格式要求,对下面这则邀请函存在的毛病进行评析。
According to the writing and format of invitation letters which you have learnt, analyze the following canonical invitation letter.

邀请函

×××集团公司:

　　为了繁荣地区经济,促进贸易交流,现定于2010年3月4日到3月7日在××市×××路×××展览中心举行商品交易会,热忱欢迎贵集团公司参加,莅临指导。如承同意,请即赐复,以便安排。

此致

敬礼

×× 市 ×× 商品展销筹备会

2010 年 2 月 4 日

附件：×× 商品展销会详细安排说明。

3 顺藤摘瓜
Follow the clues

按照例文和结构模板的提示，请自拟一则邀请函。

According to the example and templet of structure, write an invitation letter.

第十六课 感谢信
Thank-you Letter

Basic principles and aims
要点提示

1. 了解感谢信的用途。
   Understand the purposes of thank you letters.
2. 熟悉感谢信的结构和语言特点。
   Become familiar with the structure and language characteristics of thank you letters.
3. 基本掌握感谢信的写法。
   Master the basics of writing a thank you letter.

例文指路
Example guide

例文一
Example I

致《大学生》杂志社的感谢信①

《大学生》杂志社：②

　　请贵刊转告全国所有关心我的大学生、解放军战士、工人、教师及各界朋友，我的病情经几大医院治疗和各界的关心，目前已得到控制，现正在家休养。如不出意外，下学期开学即可返校学习了。

写法注释
Writing notes

① **用途及标题**：感谢信是对于关心、支援、帮助过自己的单位或个人表示感谢时使用的一种专门书信。可以公开张贴，也可以寄给单位或个人。

　　标题有三种写法，可以只写"感谢信"三个字，也可以像例文一样，写成"致×××（单位名称

第十六课 感谢信

顽疾缠身,是人生中的不幸,遭此一难,我和我的家庭几乎被摧毁了。由于《大学生》杂志的呼吁,一封封来自远方的书信、一张张几经周折转来的药方,使我那不情愿跳动的心,又恢复了正常的节奏;几乎凝滞的血,又沸腾了。一双双援助的手,一颗颗温暖的爱心,指明了我生活的路,温暖了我一家几乎冷却的心。

可敬的叔叔、阿姨、各位同学们:

我和你们天各一方,相见无期,你们却把微薄的收入,甚至把你们的助学金、生活费,或者靠卖字画得来的钱寄给了我。而你们当中甚至有人自己就有残疾,没有经济收入,你们却还献出宝贵的钱来挽救我……近来我的脑海中经常出现你们的身影。有年迈的老人,有可爱的军人,有可敬的老师,还有很多我不相识的人……我无法具体描绘你们的形象,但你们的高尚品格、助人为乐的精神将永存于我心中,永存于我家乡父老的心中……

唯一遗憾的是我不能面见答谢各位。在此请接受用你们的爱心挽救的人的深深谢意,愿你们爱的春风暖遍祖国,充满世界。

为了不辜负你们的一片爱心和良好祝愿,我将继续我的学业,继续我的事业,争取取得优异的成绩,献给关心我的远方

或个人姓名)的感谢信",如《致××报社的感谢信》。还可以由两方和文种名称组成,如《××街道致××剧院的感谢信》。

② **称谓**:写明被感谢的机关、单位、团体的名称或个人的姓名。

③ **正文**:感谢信的正文的内容一般包括以下两个部分。

第一部分先写明感谢的事由,要求用精炼的语言叙述事情的前因后果,叙述对方的好行为、好品德、好作风。要交待清楚人物、事件、时间、地点、原因、结果。

第二部分是揭示事件意义。在叙事的基础上指出对方的关心支持和帮助对整个事件或受益人的重要性,以及体现出的可贵精神,同时,表示向对方学习的态度和决心。

④ **结尾**:结尾要写上敬意的话、感谢的话,如"此致,敬礼"、"再次表示感谢"、"致以诚挚的敬意"等等。

⑤ **署名**:包括两项内容,先写明发出感谢信的单位名称或个人姓名,再注明发出感谢信的时间。

① Purpose and caption: A thank-you letter is written to an individual, group or organisation to express appreciation for their effort, support or help. It may be posted publicly or sent to them privately.

The caption may be written in three ways. It can simply include the three characters 感谢信, it can be written as 致×××的感谢信, as in the example, or it can include the writer and the recipient as in ××街道致××剧院

的各位朋友们。③

　　愿我们的心永远相通。④

贺昌玉

××××年×月×日⑤

The Thank-you Letter for the Office of "College Students" Magazine

To the Office of "College Students" Magazine:

Please pass on to all of the college students, PLA men, workers, teachers and friends who have shown me so much care, that due to their solicitude and hospital treatment my illness has been cured, and I am now resting at home. If everything progresses well, I shall soon return to school.

Being afflicted with such a persistent illness was truly a misfortune in my life, and one that almost destroyed my family and me. Due to the appeal organised by the 'College Students', I received letters from far away places, remedies that made my heart that had been unwilling to beat recover its normal rhythm; the blood that

的感谢信.

② Appellation: This should address the individual, group or organisation being thanked by name.

③ Text: This generally contains two parts. The first part details the reason for the letter, and should describe the actions of the receiver and the positive outcomes they caused. It should note the specific time and place, and be written clearly and politely.

　　The second part should talk about the overall meaning of the matter, and outline the future benefits that will occur, as well as expressing a determination to follow the good example set by the receiver.

④ Ending: Terms that express respect and appreciation should be used, for example, 此致敬礼, 再次表示感谢, 致以诚挚的敬意 etc.

⑤ Signature: This should include the name of the individual or organisation that wrote the letter, and the date of the letter's creation.

almost stopped flow rapidly again. Many pairs of helping hands and much kindness led me to find my goals in life again, and warm my family's hearts and minds that had grown cold.

Dear uncles, aunts, and every student:

We may be far apart from each other, and have little chance of meeting in the foreseeable future, yet still you have sent me your small incomes, even your stipends, your living expenses and the money you made selling paintings. Moreover, some of you are disabled men, with no income, still with your precious money you help save me...your images have been often in my mind recently. There was an old man, an adorable army man, a respected teacher, and so many others whom I don't know...I can't describe your appearance, but your noble characters, your charitable spirits only too willing to help others will be kept in my mind, and my family's minds, forever...

My only regret is that I am unable to express my appreciation to everyone in person. Please accept the grateful thanks of the man who you saved with your kindness, and who wishes that your love may be as a spring breeze, warming the whole country, and filling the world.

In order to always be worthy of your kindness and good wishes, I will continue with my studies and go on to a career, and strive to earn excellent achievements to dedicate to every friend who cared for me from afar.

I wish that our hearts and minds will always be as one,

He Changyu

Month / Day / Year

例文二
Example II

感谢信①

王××同志：②

　　您好！首先向您表示诚挚的谢意！

　　今年3月8日，我家不慎失火，情况十分危急，您作为一个过路人闻讯后立即赶赴现场，不顾自身危险，从大火中救出了我那被围困的小女儿，帮助我们扑灭了大火，避免了一场巨大损失，并且事后您分文未取，也没留下姓名和单位。经过多方打听，才得知您的地址，我们怀着无比感谢的心情写下了这封信。您这种崇高的精神值得我们学习，也值得全社会学习。在我国社会体制转轨、物欲横流、许多人一切"向钱看"的情况下，您的做法尤其难能可贵。我们对此表示衷心的感谢。

　　我们要努力做好各方面的工作，并尽力帮助需要帮助的人，以实际行动表示对您的感谢，以实际行动向您学习。③

　　此致
敬礼④

感谢人：张××
2010年3月15日⑤

写法注释
Writing notes

① **标题**：标题有三种写法，可以像本例文一样只写"感谢信"三个字。也可以写成"致×××(单位名称或个人姓名)的感谢信"，如《致××报社的感谢信》。还可以由两方和文种名称组成，如《××街道致××剧院的感谢信》。

② **称谓**：写明被感谢的机关、单位、团体的名称或个人的姓名。

③ **正文**：感谢信的正文的内容一般包括以下两个部分。

　　第一部分先写明感谢的事由，要求用精炼的语言叙述事情的前因后果，叙述对方的好行为、好品德、好作风。要交待清楚人物、事件、时间、地点、原因、结果。

　　第二部分是揭示事件意义。在叙事的基础上指出对方的关心支持和帮助对整个事件或受益人的重要性，以及体现出的可贵精神，同时，表示向对方学习的态度和决心。

④ **结尾**：结尾要写上敬意的话，感谢的话，可以像本文一样写上"此致，敬礼"，也可以写"再次表示感谢"、"致以诚挚的敬意"等等。

⑤ **署名**：包括两项内容，先写明发出感谢信的单位名称或个人姓名，再注明发出感谢信的时间。

① Caption: This may be written in three ways. It can simply include the three characters 感谢信, it can be written as 致××的感谢信,

Thank-you Letter

Comrade Wang ××:

Hello! First of all I would like to express my sincerest thanks to you!

On March 8th this year our house caught fire, and it was a very dangerous situation. As a passer-by who heard our cries for help, you rushed to help us without a thought for your own safety and saved our youngest daughter who was trapped in the fire, as well as helping us put out the fire, saving us the great loss of our house. You wouldn't take any money as a reward and didn't leave your name or address either; however after many enquiries we have finally learned your address and so are writing you this letter with unparalleled gratitude. Such a noble spirit as yours deserves to be studied and followed by us and all citizens. In this rapidly changing society filled with overflowing material desire, many people are just "chasing after money", and a spirit like yours is rare and commendable. We

as in the example, or it can include the writer and recipient as in ××街道致××剧院的感谢信.

② Appellation: This should address the individual, group or organisation being thanked by name.

③ Text: This generally contains two parts. The first part details the reason for the letter, and should describe the actions of the receiver and the positive outcomes they caused. It should note the specific time and place, and be written clearly and politely.

The second part should talk about the overall meaning of the matter, and outline the future benefits that will occur, as well as expressing a determination to follow the good example set by the receiver.

④ Ending: Terms that express respect and appreciation should be used, for example, 此致敬礼, 再次表示感谢, 致以诚挚的敬意 etc.

⑤ Signature: This should include the name of the individual or organisation who wrote the letter, and the date of the letter's creation.

109

want to convey and express our heartfelt gratitude to you.

　　We will try to do this by learning from you, and following your example by working hard to help those who need our assistance.

　　Best Wishes!

Sincerely yours: Zhang ××
March 15th, 2010

生词 New words

转告	zhuǎngào	pass on
摧毁	cuīhuǐ	destroy
周折	zhōuzhé	setback
凝滞	níngzhì	stagnate
天各一方	tiān gè yì fāng	be far apart from each other
微薄	wēibó	meagre
挽救	wǎnjiù	save
遗憾	yíhàn	regret
不慎	búshèn	carelessly
闻讯	wénxùn	hear
转轨	zhuǎnguǐ	change
物欲横流	wù yù héng liú	overflowing material desire

结构模板 The templepate of structure

致□□□□感谢信①

□□□□□□□：②

　　□□。

　　□□□□□□□□□□□□□□□□□□□□□□□□□□□□

第十六课　感谢信

　　□□□□□□□□□□□□□□□□□□。③
　此致
敬礼④

　　　　　　　　　　　　　　　　　　　　　□□□□□
　　　　　　　　　　　　　　　　　　　□□□□年□□月□□日⑤

模板格式说明

The templeate format explanation

① 标题：位置要居中。

Caption: This should be centred on the page.

② 称谓：在标题下第一行，顶格写，后面加冒号。

Appellation: Written on the line below the caption without indenting, followed by a colon.

③ 正文：段首空两格。行文中注意标点，分清层次段落。

Text: The first line should indent two spaces. Paragraphs should be arranged clearly.

④ 结尾：如果是写"此致，敬礼"，"此致"位于正文之下一行，前空两格，"敬礼"在"此致"之下顶格写。如果是"再次表示感谢"、"致以诚挚的敬意"等表示感谢的话，在正文之下一行，前空两格。

Ending: If the phrase 此致, 敬礼 is used to end the letter, then 此致 is written beneath the text and preceded by two spaces, and 敬礼 is written on the line beneath that without indenting. If another phrase, such as 再次表示感谢 or 致以诚挚的谢意 is used, then it is written on the line below the text and preceded by two spaces.

⑤ 署名：在全文右下角位置，姓名在上面一行，日期在下面一行。

Signature: This should be written at the bottom right hand side of the page. The date should be written below the signature.

1 例文评析
Example analysis

请利用你所学的感谢信的有关写作知识,对下面一则感谢信的写法、格式、内容、语言等方面进行评析。

According to the knowledge of thank-you letters which you have learnt, analyze the following thank-you letter's format, content, language, etc.

致新华路派出所的感谢信

新华路派出所:

  我是新华路39号居民张丰义。今年5月份因本人与爱人同时出差,家里只留下65岁的母亲和正上小学一年级的孩子。不料19日那天母亲下楼买菜,不慎从楼梯上摔下来,贵所李民发等几位同志正好路过,急忙将我母亲送往医院救治,还预垫了部分医疗费。之后的一个星期,这几位同志经常在百忙之中,抽空到家里来帮忙,帮助我母亲接小孩、买菜、换煤气罐等。等我们出差回来,老人和小孩都齐声夸奖贵所这几位民警,我们更是为之深深感动。

  在此,我们向贵所这几位同志表示真诚的感谢,也相信,在贵所提倡的乐于助民的口号下,本区居民的生活会越来越幸福安康!

  再次表示感谢!

  此致

敬礼

感谢人:张丰义
2009年5月30日

2 照猫画虎
Follow the model

根据下面提供的材料,按照例文和结构模板的提示,请以材料中女乘客王艳芳的名义给李华志同学写一封感谢信。

According to the following material, the example and the templet of structure, please write a thank-you letter to student Li Huazhi in name of passenger Wang Yanfang.

第十六课 感谢信

材料：

本报讯：8月27日晚上，华南师范大学学生李华志乘坐248路公交车返回学校时，在某站上来一名男子抢走女乘客王艳芳的手机，听到被抢者大呼"抓贼"后，李华志同学孤身追截，遭5名歹徒同伙围殴，其中一个歹徒手持尖刀向李华志捅过来，致使李华志右臂动脉被割断，血流不止。周围群众拨打110，李华志同学被送往华侨医院。经过4个多小时的抢救，在输入了1600毫升血液后，李华志终于脱离生命危险。医院温主任说，幸好抢救及时，否则后果不堪设想。

李华志是华南师范大学体科院体育教育专业2002级的学生。他思想上进，关心集体，富于爱心，多次向贫困生捐款。由于学习认真刻苦，成绩优良，积极参与各种活动，他被评为"社会工作积极分子"。品学兼优的他一直深受老师同学的喜爱。

连日来，《南方日报》、《广州日报》、《南方都市报》等媒体纷纷报道了李华志见义勇为的感人事迹，在社会上引起了强烈的反响。

目前，李华志已过危险期，华侨医院杨冬华院长表示，医院会组织最好的医疗力量为其救治，并给予特殊的保健营养照顾。他还表示，医院正在考虑对李华志住院期间产生的费用给予全免。

图书在版编目(CIP)数据

实用汉语写作进阶：中级：汉英对照 / 华文盛世编辑组编
北京：外文出版社，2010.12

ISBN 978-7-119-06860-2

Ⅰ．①实… Ⅱ．①华… Ⅲ．①汉语-写作-对外汉语教学-教材 Ⅳ．①H195.4

中国版本图书馆CIP数据核字(2010)第258557号

责任编辑：曲 径 孙乙鑫
装帧设计：王志刚
印刷监制：刘 刚

实用汉语写作进阶（中级）

作　者　华文盛世　编

出版发行	外文出版社有限责任公司
地　址	中国北京西城区百万庄大街24号
网　址	http://www.flp.com.cn
电　话	008610-68320579（总编室）
	008610-68995852（发行部）
印　刷	北京海纳百川旭彩印务有限公司
经　销	新华书店 / 外文书店
开　本	787mm×1092mm　1/16　印张：7.5
版　次	2011年9月第1版　第1次印刷
书　号	ISBN 978-7-119-06860-2
定　价	58.00元

邮政编码　100037
电子邮箱　flp@cipg.org.cn
008610-68327750（版权部）
008610-68996075（编辑部）

版权所有　侵权必究　如有印装问题本社负责调换（电话：008610-68995960）